Virgil's Aeneid

For Kath

Virgil's Aeneid
A Reader's Guide

David O. Ross

Blackwell Publishing

BLACKWELL PUBLISHING
350 Main Street, Malden, MA 02148-5020, USA
9600 Garsington Road, Oxford OX4 2DQ, UK
550 Swanston Street, Carlton, Victoria 3053, Australia

First published 2007 by Blackwell Publishing Ltd

1   2007

Library of Congress Cataloging-in-Publication Data

Ross, David O.
  Virgil's Aeneid : a reader's guide / David O. Ross.
    p. cm.
  Includes bibliographical references and index.
  ISBN-13: 978-1-4051-5972-2 (hardcover : alk. paper)
  ISBN-10: 1-4051-5972-3 (hardcover : alk. paper)
  ISBN-13: 978-1-4051-5973-9 (pbk. : alk. paper)
  ISBN-10: 1-4051-5973-1 (pbk. : alk. paper)
 1. Virgil. Aeneid.   I. Title.

  PA6825.R66 2007
  873′.01–dc22

                                2006025012

A catalogue record for this title is available from the British Library.

Set in 9.75 on 12.5 pt Utopia
by SNP Best-set Typesetter Ltd, Hong Kong

The publisher's policy is to use permanent paper from mills that operate a sustainable forestry policy, and which has been manufactured from pulp processed using acid-free and elementary chlorine-free practices. Furthermore, the publisher ensures that the text paper and cover board used have met acceptable environmental accreditation standards.

For further information on
Blackwell Publishing, visit our website:
www.blackwellpublishing.com

Contents

Preface

This is not a book intended for Virgilian scholars, nor on the other hand is it solely for "the general reader," who, in the area of Latin literature at least, may be as rare as the ivory-billed woodpecker. I have had in mind a fairly wide range of non-specialist readers – someone, for example, who has read Virgil in translation with some serious interest and purpose; or students, undergraduate and graduate both, who have discovered the poetry in Latin; or secondary teachers (and perhaps their students) of advanced placement courses on the *Aeneid*. Hence, citations of Virgil's text have usually been translated, with the Latin supplied only when necessary or relevant.

The *Aeneid* has always been subject to serious misunderstanding, for a number of rather obvious reasons. I hope that this brief account may make clear what Virgil's poem is *not*, and will suggest what it *is*. Many who by nature and capacity (Ezra Pound is a good example) should have understood Virgil have gotten it all wrong. Simone Weil, whose well-known essay "The *Iliad*, or the Poem of Force" is full of extraordinary insights and general perceptions of the nature of war, the nature of violence, and humanity, has only this to say of Virgil's revisiting of Homer: "the *Aeneid* is an imitation which, however brilliant, is disfigured by frigidity, bombast, and bad taste." How sad. Everything she says about the *Iliad* could as aptly be said of Virgil's epic.

For a while I thought I was writing an "Introduction" to Virgil, but I found out, finally, that I wasn't. Introductions exist, with the facts of Virgil's life, with book-by-book plot outlines of the *Aeneid*, and with some sort of literary explication. (The best of these is still W. F. Jackson Knight's *Roman Vergil* [London, 1944], published over sixty years ago.) I came to realize, rather, that I was writing a "Guide" to the *Aeneid*, something that might help the sort of reader I had in mind to find a way into what really matters in such a great poem, at least as I have come to read it.

This guide will explore some parts of the poem in more detail than some readers will want to follow. Tours of Book V, for example, or of the shield in Book VIII, or of the *Eclogues* need not be taken or followed to the end, but their purpose is to present in some detail something essential about Virgil's poetry. On the other hand, there are certain general explorations here of areas such as Roman religion or Roman conceptions of character; these too are not intended as introductions (which obviously they cannot be), but rather, again, as guides to important aspects of Virgil's poetry. A good tour guide is one who is not compelled to reel off, exhaustively, all the dates, facts, and points of interest about an object or a site, but who can illuminate what is essential, providing a way of seeing and putting together certain selected pieces in a meaningful and suggestive manner, and I hope I have been able to do this for Virgil.

I have tried to avoid all polemic, which does not mean that I have put aside my obvious biases or aimed at a neutral objectivity. I have thought it best to avoid footnotes and bibliography altogether: once started, there is no stopping, and taking sides in the recent Virgil wars becomes unavoidable. I am obviously indebted to the work of others, and apologize to those who will recognize what is their own, unacknowledged. The reader who wants further readings on Virgil will find them easily: there are good and readily available collections of essays and scholarly articles, as well as the "introductions" mentioned above, all with footnotes and bibliographies.

I have added an appendix on meter, since it is my impression that there exists considerable misunderstanding of how the Latin hexameter works, and to hear Virgil's verse improperly is to miss a great deal. Again, the appendix is very selective. Latin metrics is a difficult subject. Eduard Norden's monumental edition of Book VI of the *Aeneid* (4th edn., Stuttgart, 1957), for instance, has valuable appendices on meter and other stylistic features, but little of the rich feast he offers is to be had in a more digestible form. (One exception is L. P. Wilkinson's *Golden Latin Artistry* [Cambridge, 1963].)

I would like to thank *il professore* Warren Myers (once again) and Andres Reyes, both of whom read and commented on the final draft. Richard Thomas and Barbara Weiden Boyd also found time, somehow, to offer valuable corrections and suggestions. Special thanks are due to Henry Walters, who read a first draft, saw that it was thoroughly misconceived, and was able to open my eyes to the necessity of a total rewriting, which, two years later, he also had the patience to read: *gratias tibi maximas ago.*

At each stage (school, college, and graduate study) I was fortunate to read Virgil with extraordinary teachers, whom I have often been thinking about as I have been writing these pages: Russell A. Edwards, Lawrence Richardson, and Wendell Clausen. No expression of thanks could begin to be adequate.

All the writing of this book was done at the Groton School, where I found a happy refuge in retirement. I thank two headmasters, William Polk and Richard Commons, for allowing me to continue to teach, and the faculty and students for the stimulation of conversation and community.

All citations of Virgil's text are from the Oxford Classical Text of R. A. B. Mynors (1972). The utilitarian translations are my own, either awkwardly precise or a loose paraphrase, as required.

Peterborough, NH

Introduction

What is most obvious often receives the least attention, and then details can dominate, distorting or obscuring the whole, as in the story of the three blind men and the elephant. What is most obvious about Virgil's *Aeneid* is that it is based on Homer's two great epics in its broadest structure, in some of its major episodes and minor panels, and even in so many details of diction and meter. The *Iliad* is the great poem of war, and the *Odyssey* of the restoration of peace – that is, the return from war and the re-establishment of the social order, family, and home. Whatever their origins, this is the way the Homeric epics were viewed in antiquity and are still seen today.

It was immediately obvious to Virgil's readers that the first half of his poem, both generally and in detail, is set against the backdrop of the *Odyssey*, the wanderings on land and sea of the hero, driven by angered divinity; the second half replays the scenes of war of the *Iliad*. "*Arma virumque cano*," Virgil began, just as Homer had begun with "the wrath" (*menin*, the first word of the *Iliad*) and "the hero" (*andra*, the first word of the *Odyssey*) – details obvious enough.

It should be perfectly obvious, then – and it has been to many readers – that Virgil's poem is a complete inversion of Homer. In its narrative chronology it begins with the destruction of Troy, which necessitates Aeneas' seven years of wandering. Whereas Odysseus, "much-enduring," finally returns to the Ithaca of his birth, to father, son, and his wife's bed, Aeneas, the "pious" hero, begins with the loss of his city and his beloved wife, setting out to find some new home that he cannot know and that he will not, in fact, establish by the poem's end, and losing his father on the way. Viewed against the *Odyssey*, the *Aeneid* is a poem of loss. In the *Iliad* the wrath of Achilles finds its resolution in the return of Hector's corpse to Priam and in the funeral rites for Patroclus. The Iliadic half of the *Aeneid* ends with an act of madness and terrible anger, Aeneas' slaying of Turnus. Here there is no resolution.

Another broad view is offered right at the start, by Virgil himself, in the conventional proemium. "I sing of war and a hero," who came from Troy to Italy, beginning the succession of men and events that will lead to the lofty walls of Rome. The *Aeneid* is about a historical process, extending even to Virgil's own day. When his readers listen to Jupiter's predictions in Book I, or see the parade of the *clarissimi viri* in Book VI or the scenes on the shield in Book VIII, they are reading, in these revelations of Aeneas' future, about their own past. Again, obvious enough. The *Aeneid* is a poem of time, just as the *Eclogues* had been concerned with the creation of physical space and the *Georgics* had set the farmer's world in both dimensions.

From the shores of Troy to the walls of Rome: Aeneas exists between the Trojan past, destroyed forever in the blind darkness of a single night, and the future that he himself will never have and can know of only vaguely, through images that he can only dimly comprehend. He is a hero deprived of his past, to which, in contrast with Odysseus, he cannot return, and on a mission to some future that he will never have a part of. This, again, should be obvious.

But what may be less clear is Virgil's insistence on the deceptiveness of the images of the hero's past and future. The painted scenes of the Trojan war on Juno's temple at Carthage that Aeneas gazes at with so much emotion are scenes of the reality of war, but they are only "an empty representation" (*pictura inani*, 1.464). And the Troy in Book III so carefully restored by Andromache is only a monument to what is dead, totally devoid of any reality or substance. For Virgil, the images that we hold of our past can never be real. What we hope for the future is equally illusory, with even less substance. Again, what is shown to Aeneas of the Rome to come – the ghostly figures in the Underworld and the scenes on the shield that he can only "wonder at in ignorance" (8.730) – is the reader's past, just as subject to distortion as is Aeneas' future.

If so much is obvious, how can we see the *Aeneid* simply as a gift to the Roman people of their own Homeric epic – perhaps even greater than the *Iliad*, as Propertius ecstatically hailed it (2.34.66)? How can a poem that so consistently and emphatically deals in the deceptive images of past and future be read as nothing more than a glorification of the progress from Troy to the Augustan *imperium*?

One way to answer these questions also seems to me obvious. Readers of the *Aeneid* tend to forget that Virgil was a poet. This may be because modern readers often come to the *Aeneid* through a translation, where little of the poetry can survive. Or, perhaps, if they have experienced some of the poem in Latin, they may not have come to it from the *Eclogues* and *Georgics*, both thoroughly and supremely the works of a poet. Even so, Virgil as a poet is not easily accessible, just as, for example, T. S. Eliot is not easily accessible. I do not mean that he is an obscure or "difficult" poet, as Eliot can be, but his poetry depends so often on allusion, in often rather subtle ways, to his poetic inheritance. Without an acquaintance with the poets and contexts to which Virgil alludes, we will miss a great deal, inevitably, but so it must be. Very little attention, therefore, can be paid in what follows to such predecessors as the Alexandrians Theocritus or Apollonius, or to Catullus and the neoteric poets of the preceding generation, except for mention of broad themes and content, though I hope something can be suggested.

But Virgil has been read for centuries during which Latin and its literature were understood, and still the *Aeneid* has been seen as a grand boast, a justification of the Roman mission. *Prima facie*, of course, it is just that, and for many readers there is no point in going further. False confidence comes from what we think we know, and at that point we stop thinking. There are the gods, recognizable, supreme, either directing fate and Rome's destiny or at least the agents of a universal order. Likewise throughout the poem we can see and even identify various strands of philosophical import, giving us again a confidence that we are getting Virgil's message, reducible to Stoic or other doctrine. But Virgil was a poet, not a historian, a political apologist, a theologian, or a philosopher.

There are, of course, philosophers who write in verse, like Lucretius, and that work of magnificent poetry, *Paradise Lost*, is theological, without a doubt. But a poet like Virgil is not in the business of solving problems and offering solutions. A historian, social scientist, or philosopher argues deductively from evidence to arrive at an answer, or at least a theoretically satisfying conclusion, to show (it may be) that the Roman achievement, fore-ordained, was justified at whatever the cost. Virgil, as I will argue, had no such agenda. The world he creates is imaginative, not discursive and reasoned: none of his poems ends with a conclusion, an apophoretic message to take away with us. Poetic meaning cannot be caught in the net of analysis, typified, catalogued, and stored away systematically in its proper drawer of a critical cabinet. The *Aeneid* does have meaning, but it has no answers.

If we read the *Aeneid* for answers, we will inevitably miss the obvious. Virgil never asks whether Aeneas was right to abandon Dido for the sake of a nobler cause, or whether Turnus' death was just or divinely ordered. He shows us certain actions: Aeneas suddenly leaves Carthage at divine urging, with no other explanation but with tragic results; Turnus dies like

Camilla and, in fact, like Patroclus and Hector. The meaning, though, is never simple, nor should we want it to be. The poet connects, shows us ambiguities that can result from the connections he has made, and creates a web of human experience that is far richer than any solution could ever be.

The inversion of the Homeric narratives is the concept of a poet, just as is the vision of the hero existing in an emptiness between past and future. Images are all that Aeneas has, and they are all that Virgil, as a poet, has to work with. Not coincidentally is Virgil a remarkably visual poet, who sees not just scenes but movement. It has been pointed out that Catullus' scenes are static, as if he had in mind a painting, but that Virgil often follows the development of a scene as if through the lens of a cinema camera. Our eye follows from one image directly to another and on to another. When (for example) Neoptolemus breaks a hole in the massive doors of Priam's palace, we look with him through the "window" (*fenestram*) he has made, down through the atrium, down through the inner rooms (*penetralia*) and on to the inner courtyard, and finally, as if in a close-up now, to the terrified human figures (2.481–90). Virgil is a visual poet, and in this new, cinematic way. But he is also far closer to Homer, in the way he sees, than any other ancient poet, I think. Homer had no language for reasoned analysis, for logical argument leading to a right or wrong: he can only show us *what* he sees, *what* his heroes do and say, not *why* they reason as they do. We may see a Homeric hero on occasion pondering formulaically, but, other than offering a few alternatives for action, he does not allow us into his head. If Homer wants to show us an act of irrational passion, for instance, he must say that a hero was *like* a lion driven by hunger to enter a farm yard. Visual art does not achieve its effects through logic and reason.

Because Virgil is a visual poet, he does not offer answers and solutions, nor does he tell us what he means, because to do so would be to negate the power and the very nature of visual art. The images themselves and the flow of images into each other are what convey his meaning, and this meaning, like that of Homer, cannot be reduced to words, to a bland paraphrase. Take, as an example, a scene that we will revisit later in more detail. In Book I Aeneas meets his mother for the first time, as he sets out to see what sort of land the storm has driven them to. What sort of goddess is this, and what sort of mother, who appears to her son only in disguise? A variety of answers has been offered, because Virgil gives no conclusion of his own. Instead, he shows us Aeneas' immediate reaction, in his own words, as his goddess-mother turns from him and leaves (1.407–9). The power of this devastating moment could have been achieved in no other way.

The *Aeneid* is not concerned with morality, with questions of demonstrable right and wrong. If we allow ourselves to be caught up in such discussions, we risk reducing Virgil's poetic complexity to an insensitive simplicity. Virgil was a poet.

Virgil may be close to Homer in his sense of the visual image, but there is a world of difference between the two in other respects. The poet of the *Iliad* and *Odyssey* comes at the end of a long succession of oral singers going back to the bards we see in the *Odyssey*, Phemius and Demodocus, and to Achilles himself, singing in his tent "the famous deeds of men." The Homeric poems are oral compositions, or "primary" epic, behind which stand generations of singers, using an inherited set of poetic formulae, epithets, and words to fit every metrical need, fluid and ever-changing. This tradition, and the ability to compose orally, came to an end with the use of alphabetic writing in the seventh century BC, though precisely how remains unclear.

"Secondary" epic (that is, literary or written) is an entirely different animal. No epics of any significance were composed in Greece after Homer: his precedent was overwhelming, beyond emulation in both matter and manner. The old heroes appear on the tragic stage at Athens, but who could even imagine writing like Homer? Eventually, though, in the third century BC a small group of poets associated with the great library at Alexandria experimented with a "short epic," and Apollonius of Rhodes composed a learned and allusive *Argonautica* (the story of Jason) in four lengthy books. These were scholar-poets (Callimachus, Theocritus, Aratus, Apollonius, and others) for whom learning and the exquisitely polished miniature were the goal. Homer returns, not to be imitated but as the source for an obscure word or a recherché reference. Their model was not Homer, but Hesiod, his supposed contemporary.

The Homeric hexameter comes to Rome with Quintus Ennius (239–169 BC), but he and his successors (such as Naevius) used it only for annalistic history: Ennius' *Annales* told the story of Rome from its beginnings to 171 BC in 18 books, in an artificial diction and foreign meter, imitating the style of Homer in mannerisms of diction and meter that by Virgil's time seemed rough and uncouth. Though translations and staging of Greek tragedy were a flourishing concern, what little there was of epic at Rome continued to be historical. Then, suddenly, there was the *Aeneid*: it takes an effort to realize just what an extraordinary innovation this was. Any serious poet at Rome at this time, following Catullus and his friends in the preceding generation, was a devoted adherent of Callimachean principles, of the short poem polished with style and learning, for whom a long poem on "kings and battles" (such as the historical epic of Ennius) was an anathema. Virgil had begun with Theocritus as his model for the *Eclogues* and Aratus (and Hesiod) for the *Georgics*, but the *Aeneid* was both Homeric and Ennian. Nothing could have seemed more reactionary, more of a betrayal of poetic principles.

But what was by far the most important discovery of these Alexandrians – more important than their learning or craftsmanship – was how to reduce the old heroes and their great deeds to human scale. Apollonius' Jason and Medea are subject to passions and faults all too human. Jason appears often as an incompetent, a bumbler, and a cad, and Medea is both the witch of towering passion and supernatural powers (as she had been for Euripides) and also a naïve girl experiencing love for the first time. For the Alexandrians, erotic passion is the key, as if the old heroes had given up combat for love. For Catullus and the new poets, the discovery of Alexandrian poetics opened a way to put the individual back into poetry and at the same time to transform personal experience through poetic abstraction, elevating the personal by setting it against a grander tradition. Catullus' Ariadne (in poem 64) is recognizably Apollonius' Medea, but she is even more a distillation of the poet's own experience of betrayal and abandonment and thus, as a poetic abstraction, she becomes a far more powerful expression of his disillusionment than anything to be found in his shorter, more direct, poems.

All of this, now, comes directly down to the *Aeneid*. What a Homeric-Ennian epic offered Virgil was a new dimension of expression, never imagined before and never, with the possible exception of *Paradise Lost*, realized since, I think. Virgil now had access to the remotest literary past of both Greece and Rome, which could be used to produce the richness and solemnity of an organ in a great cathedral. Homer (and the later appearances of his heroes in Greek tragedy) supplied not only the grand paradigms of heroic struggle and death, but, in his lighter moments, an irreverent playfulness as well. The Homeric-Ennian precedent, too, could often provide a backdrop for a scene, exploited by Virgil in a variety of ways, but most frequently and effectively to mark a contrast with the Alexandrian or Catullan hero, an individual of human scale, who is playing his part in front of the epic scenery.

One example might make this clear.

The singers who preceded Homer over a period of four centuries or more had one thing in common with the grandmothers over a far longer span of time who, sitting by the cottage fireplace, passed on our European stock of fairy tales: story-telling. The Greek bards knew how to hold their listeners with the spell of their stories, whether like Phemius and Demodocus they entertained their lords at the feast, or whether, like the succession of traveling singers who passed on and continually renewed the rich stock of heroic legends, they performed (as we can imagine) in the squares of towns and villages. Homeric narrative, consequently, is strikingly different from the sophisticated literary narrative of secondary epic, in this respect: it is realistic, with the realism demanded by children listening to a fairy tale. Every detail must be precise and logical. What happens may be completely fantastic: pigs in fact may fly, but every step of the narrative must be rationally justified, and no step can be left out.

In Book X of the *Odyssey*, Odysseus (who is himself the story-teller at this point) lands with his single remaining ship on an unknown shore, barely having escaped from the Laestrygonians. His men lie there, resting and grieving, for two days and nights; at the third dawn Odysseus, alone (as Homer finds necessary to mention), climbs a rocky peak to look for signs of human habitation. Not quite: Homer adds a detail before Odysseus sets out, that he takes a spear. Do we need to know this? Is this simply a formulaic convention, of no more significance than the "rosy-fingered" that always accompanies the dawn? This is what happens, after he catches sight of the smoke rising from what will prove to be Circe's hall. (I translate as literally as possible.)

> But when, as I came down, I was near my curved ship,
> just then some god took pity on me, being alone,
> and sent for me a great stag, lofty-antlered, in my very path.
> He was going from a wooded pasture to the river
> to drink, for the heat of the sun was upon him.
> I struck him as he came forth in the spine in mid-back,
> and the bronze spear went right through.
> He fell in the dust bellowing, and his life-breath flew forth.
> I stepped upon him and drew my bronze spear from the wound,
> and I leaned it then upon the ground and left it there.
> Then I gathered up some vines and withies
> and, weaving a rope a fathom long, well-plaited all around,
> I bound up the feet of the huge beast.
> I went, carrying him slung over behind my neck, to the black ship,
> leaning on my spear, since it wasn't possible to carry him
> on one shoulder with the other hand, for he was indeed a huge buck.
> (*Od.* 10.156–71)

The details are striking. Odysseus in his descent has come very near the shore: we will need to remember later that he won't have far to go, carrying that weight. Some god, yes, has sent this huge stag to cross his path, but immediately a more natural explanation is offered: the sun was hot, the buck thirsty and on the way to the river to drink. Note that the stag was just emerging from the wood (and therefore hadn't yet sensed Odysseus). Now we see why the narrator mentioned the spear at the very beginning. The details of precisely where the spear hit and how the buck bellowed and died are typical of Homer's realism. How do you pull a spear from a body? By "going upon it," presumably, that is, using one foot to pull against. He then "leans the spear upon the ground" – that is, he left it right at hand, upright, and we will soon see why. We now remember that he had set out "alone," and that is precisely his difficulty. But he weaves some vines into a rope of just the right length, ties the animal's feet together, heaves him up across his back with the tied feet in front, and, with the help of the carefully positioned spear, carries him to the ship, which wasn't far away.

This sort of narrative detail is typical of Homer. Certain details, to be sure, are there simply because of the formulaic nature of oral poetry (the spear is "bronze," the ship is "curved" or "black"), and all the details of the killing (lines 161–5) appear in separate scenes of slaughter in the *Iliad* and can thus be seen as the stock-in-trade of the oral poet. But there is a realism here that is almost naïve: a six-year-old always wants to know precisely how.

See now what Virgil did with this scene. Aeneas, with a numerically more satisfying seven ships, has survived the great storm at the beginning of Book I, driven to an unknown shore. He climbs a convenient peak, to look for his lost ships and men.

> No ship was in sight, but he saw three stags
> wandering on the shore. These were followed by whole herds
> from behind, and the long line grazes through the valley.
> He took a stand there and took in hand the bow and swift arrows
> which faithful Achates bore,
> and laid low first the leaders of the herd, their heads lofty
> with tree-like antlers, then routed in confusion the pack, the whole herd,
> driving them with his weapons in the leafy wood,
> nor did he stop before, triumphant, he had dropped seven huge bodies
> to the ground, equaling the number of his ships.
> Thence he returns to the port and shares out the booty to his men.
> (*Aen.* 1.184–94)

We are in an entirely different poetic world here, which Virgil, setting the contrast with Homer, wants us to be aware of. This is poetry in the grand style. There are the required epithets ("faithful" Achates, "tree-like" antlers). A military metaphor runs through the whole passage – this is poetry, not realism. Aeneas remains isolated and superior to it all on the peak, the deer far below on a grand stage. Not one buck, but three appear, and these are followed by whole herds that fill the valley. Aeneas seizes his armament from the faithful Achates (the first we hear of him – Homer would certainly have prepared us) and, with a rain of arrows, drives the herd in a rout of confusion more suggestive of the firepower of a modern army than of a single archer. But the greatest embarrassment is still to come: without any explanation these "seven huge bodies" are down on the shore.

The contrast with Homer is clear. Homer's presentation is simplicity itself. Virgil's scene is what we have come to expect in secondary epic. There is a grandeur, a solemnity, which C. S. Lewis in *A Preface to Paradise Lost* has compared to the ceremonial pomp of a coronation or a high church service. The heroic has become magnified to the point that the hero himself has become faceless. Aeneas takes no pride, and certainly no joy, in what he has done, as had Odysseus: it is all performance, acted out on a stage vast and elaborately set, but so far away that we can see no expression on the actor's face.

It would seem to be Virgil who discovered this solemnity, and certainly he developed and exploited its possibilities. Secondary epic begins with him, and it was from Virgil, not from Homer, that Milton and others learned. Yet how empty and tedious this grandeur can seem to be, and how mechanical such a faceless hero can appear. But this is the very purpose of ceremonial pomp, to erase what is human and individual in its participants: we see only the archbishop with his robes, not the real man beneath, and we do not want to know what he had for breakfast.

It is clear to me that Virgil thought a great deal about this solemnity, because every time he sets a scene on this grand scale, something human is about to be revealed, some pain that we are too far away to see on the actor's face, some suffering deep within the heart beneath the golden vestments, some anguish that the pomp of the occasion must necessarily conceal. After Aeneas has distributed the seven deer, one to each ship, he offers his men words of encouragement, exactly as had Odysseus (the model is still before us) and in much the same words: "Perhaps at some future time we will be pleased to recall even this distress" (*forsan et haec olim meminisse iuvabit*, 1.203). But then, suddenly, in the next two lines the Homeric model is left behind and the human being is revealed: "Such are his words, and sick at heart with immense grief he feigns hope in his expression, but hides his pain deep in his heart" (*talia voce refert curisque ingentibus aeger / spem vultu simulat, premit altum corde dolorem*, 1.208–9).

It is easy to miss these moments, because Virgil does not often allow his hero to have them: Aeneas must for the most part be the hero of the new mission. But if he still seems wooden, mechanical, inhuman, a mere puppet on strings worked by the gods, perhaps we are too awed by the pomp of the ceremonial procession.

Virgil has written a poem not so much about Rome's origins and its imperial present, but about the deceptive images that we continually make and remake to restore our past and imagine our future. There is no other way we can live, as a people or as individuals. These are the images too of his poetry, constantly altering, reappearing in new associations with each other throughout the epic, and reaching back to earlier poets and other contexts. These images do not allow us easy conclusions about right and wrong, good and bad: they show us only how the world is, and that is the deep sadness of it all, the Virgilian tears.

Aeneas' experience is of loss, the loss of home, family, and whatever is most dear to him; he is a hero denied all human contact because of the grand and glorious mission. When we see him first, at the height of the storm, his wish is to have died at Troy, and when we see him next, we realize that, as a hero, he is not allowed to express his human grief – *premit altum corde dolorem*. But it is there to see, again and again, in his anguish and tears at every loss, when, for just a brief moment, we are allowed a glimpse at the real face behind the actor's mask.

1

Virgil's Hero

The traditional hero stands half-way between the gods and men. Many of Homer's heroes have a divine parent, as does Aeneas, and often a god will take their side in battle, helping or protecting. For Homer and his audience, any act that seems to surpass human capability or that violates the norms and expectations of accepted behavior can be attributed to divine intervention, as when Athene on occasion prompts Odysseus, or when she stays Achilles' hand as he is about to draw his sword against Agamemnon in the first book of the *Iliad*. In the Homeric epics, divine intervention is often a way of presenting or abstracting an instance of human behavior that appears superhuman, unexpected, or deviant.

When this intersection of the divine and human is taken literally, though, a problem arises which nothing less than genius can overcome. The problem is simple: a heroic figure who becomes too superhuman is of little interest. We easily tire of reading about the exploits of heroes who never fail, no matter how dire the struggle becomes, in epics where even final defeat and death are only transfiguration and glory. The sagas of Iceland, Scandinavia, Finland, or Ireland are read today mainly by those who have a nationalistic motivation or a specialist interest, and the Nibelung saga lives on largely through Wagner's genius. Transcendent achievement, by itself, doesn't satisfy for very long, simply because in its contact with the divine it loses what is human.

We all know, though, what it is to be human because we live with it every day, and hence the mundane experience of ordinary people living their everyday lives can become of literary interest only when given a significance that removes the experience from the everyday, that makes it mean something more. Good stories have always been about the transforming experience (when Jack gets his beans or the elves visit the shoemaker), in an unreal setting (an enchanted forest or the realm at the top of the beanstalk), with the grant of a magical token (a harp, a herb, a wand, a ring) that bestows supernatural and therefore very dangerous power on the weakest or lowliest among us. The epic hero, if he is to move us deeply, must be thoroughly human when that bright light of god-sent glory comes upon him.

We need literature, then, to show us ourselves when we experience a moment of greatness, when we can realize that there is something within us that is transcendent, that is shared with divinity, but we know too that the glory can only exist for a moment, because to be human is to experience failure and suffer defeat. Willie Loman (in Arthur Miller's *Death of a Salesman*) is no common man, in spite of what we are so often told: he is not simply a failed salesman, for if he were, he would be simply pathetic. He is as heroic a figure as Oedipus or Lear, a man who once was the best and who lived a dream of glory even in failure, and it is Miller's genius to make us feel this again and again throughout the play. Willie even communicates with the divine, hearing Ben's call to step into another world entirely, to leave the human sphere behind. The hero must do great deeds and must excel, but if he is to move us and have meaning, he must also fail, because failure is human, and the most human failure is death. It is our mortality that distinguishes us from the gods, who live forever.

Aeneas has had a long history of being misunderstood and misrepresented, usually for the same reason. Unlike Willie Loman, Aeneas has been taken to be a hero who has left behind, or perhaps never had, any trace of our shared humanity, who has joined forces with, or even sold out to, the gods and a national destiny. It is easy enough to see how this has been and still very often is his misfortune. Once the assumption is made that the *Aeneid* is the national epic of Rome, it follows that Virgil could only have seen the grandeur and the glory in Rome's triumphant progress to the Augustan empire, to the rule of law and peace throughout the world. Given that and Aeneas' remarkable piety, what else could there be to this Augustan hero? Virgil, in this view, has created a mere emblematic automaton, a wooden puppet lacking in genuine human emotion; the epic itself can be of interest only to "those who have a nationalistic motivation or a specialist interest"; and the case can be closed.

Three Scenes of Crisis

We can begin by considering three scenes that could well lead to or support such a conclusion. All three scenes show the hero at a moment of crisis and indecision. Such moments are not uncommon in Homer, who had formulae at hand to describe a hero thinking deeply in his heart, pondering a course of action "in his reflective diaphragm." The difference between a Homeric hero at a time of crisis and Aeneas is simply this, that in Homer the hero then acts, decisively and without further hesitation, whereas for Aeneas there is no course of action possible, no way to resolve the conflict.

First scene (2.634–704)

Troy has fallen. Aeneas has just been a spectator at Priam's murder, and Venus has revealed to him the gods at their work of destruction. She urges flight as an end to further struggle and promises her assistance.

But when he returns home, he finds his father refusing to leave his city: he is too old, he says, and he has seen Troy laid low once before; he is ready to die, even without proper burial. The whole family's tearful appeal moves him not at all, and Aeneas is left with no choice but to seek again death in arms – pointless, but heroic ("Not without revenge will we all die today," 2.670).

As Aeneas resumes his arms and starts to leave the house, Virgil replays, with characteristic brevity, Hector's final departure from Troy in *Iliad* Book VI, as he met his wife and infant son at the Scaean Gate. Andromache's appeal is entirely personal, directly human: why should he abandon those closest to him, why return to combat and death? Hector's answer is one of Homer's clearest revelations of the futility and tragedy of traditional heroism, "the heroic code" (as we too easily call it): he knows no other way, he would feel shame before his people if he did not fight, but, as he thinks of the day that he knows must come to his city, he grieves most deeply for his wife's inevitable fate. Then we have another of Homer's extraordinary moments, a simple visual presentation of a complex of emotions for which there were no words, and for which we too have no words nearly as effective. Astyanax, in his nurse's arms, cries out in fright as his father reaches out to him, and Hector removes his great horse-haired helmet, the very emblem of his heroism, to take his son into his arms for the last time. And yet all that Hector can do, all that he knows to say, is to pray that Astyanax will some day be the warrior that his father was, or even better, in the eyes of his people, and will delight his mother as he brings home the bloody armor of his slain enemy.

The scene was to be replayed often (as, for example, by Sophocles in the *Ajax*), since in its extraordinary details it is the most perfect representation of the opposition between heroic duty and the claims of personal love. The tension between the futility of heroic death and human obligation has never yet been resolved. Virgil needs only to suggest the Homeric scene,

as Creusa embraces Aeneas' knees and holds out to him the infant Ascanius (*parvum*, 674; *parvus*, 677) to set this conflict directly before us.

At this point, then, we see Aeneas as a Homeric hero, or more specifically, as Hector, presented with the fundamental opposition that Homer
was the first (we may feel sure) to pose, and which he posed again on
several other occasions in his great poem – the futility of heroism and its
cost in human terms. At this point in the *Aeneid* a crisis has been reached,
and Aeneas has no other response to make than Hector had. As he
stands there, facing his wife and son, we know that he too will go on to
a senseless death in what he knows, and has been told by Venus, is a
lost cause.

But the moment of inaction brought on by Creusa's appeal is unexpectedly resolved before Aeneas can act. Fire springs from Iulus' head, harmlessly. Anchises prays for a confirming sign, and thunder is heard on the
left and a shooting star flames across the sky and disappears behind
Mount Ida. For the Roman reader, Iulus' fire means imperial power to
come, and the shooting star is none other than the *sidus Iulium*, the comet
that appeared in the summer of 44 BC, identified immediately by the young
Octavian as confirming the immortality of his adoptive father.

The dramatic crisis, and Homer's opposition, are resolved, and no
choice is necessary for Virgil's hero. From this point on in the narrative
chronology Aeneas assumes another, entirely new, dimension. He will
continue, of course, to play the role of a Homeric hero, with all the tensions implicit in that role, but he will be the hero of Virgil's national epic.
As he assumes this new purpose, what is required of him first is flight, to
abandon the hero's only response, death in fighting for his city. He will then
be called upon to accept the loss of his beloved wife.

Second scene (5.700–45)

The games in honor of Anchises have been held, games which are in effect
a return to Troy. Caesar's comet recurs as the climax of the final contest,
after which the Trojan youth stage the equestrian display, the *ludus
Troianus*, that will be part of the Augustan restoration of Rome's Trojan
origin. Book V is a transition.

The women have been engaged in a separate ceremony at Anchises'
tomb. Juno, taking advantage of their weariness, sends Iris, who, appearing as the distinguished matron Beroe, appeals to their longing for a
re-established Troy and induces them to burn their ships. The timely intervention of Ascanius, though, and the prayer of Aeneas to Jupiter, produces
a sudden thunderstorm. The fire is miraculously extinguished, with the
loss of only four ships.

One would think that such a miracle occurring in response to a prayer would be a welcome sign, confirming both the gradual revelation of the mission in Book III and Mercury's delivery of Jupiter's commands that precipitated the flight from Carthage and Dido. Why then does Aeneas at this moment struggle with heroic doubt (700–3), "turning over in his mind his great cares, now here, now there, whether to remain in Sicily, forgetful of fate, or to go on to Italy"? Why this indecision? Virgil insists that we take notice. A Trojan elder, one Nautes, who never appears elsewhere, is brought on to offer what would seem to be the obvious solution – to let the weak, weary, and fearful remain in Sicily under Acestes' care (thus solving the problem of the four destroyed ships), while the rest get on with it. Simplicity itself, it would seem.

Not at all. "Then, aroused by the words of his old friend, [Aeneas] is indeed divided, reflecting on all his cares" (719–20). It is midnight, and Anchises appears before him (there is no indication of sleep or a dream), claiming to be sent by Jupiter and commanding obedience to Nautes' advice. He briefly announces the necessity of the journey to the Under-world, where the Roman future will be revealed, and then disappears (as had Eurydice from Orpheus, *Geo.* 4.499–500) "like smoke into thin air," insubstantial, escaping his son's embrace. We are reminded of Creusa's ghost: both the beloved wife and dear father have lost their human reality and have become the impersonal interpreters of divine design and imperial destiny.

Considering the scene as a whole, what we see, again, is a moment of crisis and indecision. Virgil's repetition of the Homeric formulae of doubt, when a hero ponders on a course of action, is to be noted. What may not be evident at first (that is, just why Aeneas is so hesitant, when the proper course of action is so obvious to Nautes and indeed to us) becomes clear in the larger context of the Book: on the one hand, the desperate longing for Troy and the past and, on the other, the weariness of the seven years of wandering and the uncertainty of the future. No Homeric hero, even Odysseus, was ever so conflicted.

Third scene (4.279–95)

Another moment of crisis occurs at Carthage after Mercury's appearance to Aeneas, relaying Jupiter's commands. Again it is signaled by the Homeric formulae of indecision and reflection: "[Aeneas] casts his mind swiftly now here, now there, considers different options, and explores all possibilities" (4.285–6).

It has become a clear case of dereliction of duty. Jupiter lays it out, with as much exasperation as his dignity and epic diction permit, when he gives his instructions to Mercury (223–37), and Mercury, in the Homeric manner, repeats the accusations to Aeneas (265–76): while he lingers in Carthage, an enemy land, he has forgotten that he is the hero of a Roman epic, denying all that is owed to Iulus, all the glory of Roman citadels. There is a further detail here worth noting. Mercury finds Aeneas not only engaged in the actual building of Carthage (bad enough), but armed with a display sword, "studded with tawny jasper," and wearing a Tyrian purple cloak, "which wealthy Dido had made as a gift, weaving in a thread of gold" (259–64). Wealth, gold, jeweled arms, Tyrian purple – all very foreign, barbaric, and un-Roman. This is how it appears to Olympian divinity, but this is not at all what Virgil wants us to conclude. We will see Dido's work again, when Aeneas clothes Pallas' corpse, "as a supreme honor," with one of the two cloaks which Dido had made with her own hands, happy in her work, "weaving in a thread of gold" (11.73–5). When Virgil repeats full lines, it is always significant: the immediate context of laying out Pallas' body is rich with direct allusions to Catullan themes of the senseless destruction of the delicate and beautiful.

Dido too is a Catullan figure, who will be destroyed, like Ariadne, by a foreign hero and by the heroic world, and the process is about to begin. This is not the occasion to review such details, but Aeneas' indecisiveness cannot be understood without appreciating that Dido, while in the eyes of Jupiter, Venus, and Roman destiny the enemy *par excellence*, is for Virgil the object of tragic sympathy, beyond all others. This is the opposition that Aeneas again finds himself torn by, and at this point it is only this opposition that concerns Virgil. Consider carefully just what happens – what Virgil tells us and what he doesn't – in this extraordinarily condensed passage of crisis, indecision, reflection, and action, for once, taken.

Aeneas is dumbstruck. Mercury's appearance, in broad daylight, is no dream. The hero's hair bristles in horror, his voice sticks in his throat (279–80). He immediately, without questions and without reflection, accepts the command of Jupiter – "he is fired with the desire to be off and to leave this dear land" (*dulcis . . . terras*, 281). Whether he should leave was not for a moment in question: at this point there is no crisis, no hesitation or indecision. If ever there is a justification for seeing Aeneas as a puppet of the gods, a wooden automaton, this is it. But Virgil has no interest, at this moment, in any of our concerns with romantic motivation; he has not a word of apology to make to us, should we want to know how, or even why, Aeneas can so abruptly, so inhumanly, deny his obligations to Dido, much less his love for her. It is only the fact of the matter that Virgil is concerned with, and the fact, at this point, is the simple opposition between some grand, controlling order of the universe and individual human suffering.

We must accept, then, that Aeneas has suddenly been restored to his role as the hero of a proper Roman epic, and his is not to reason why. Yet we ought to note that his first thoughts and concerns are all for Dido. "What should he do? With what words could he dare to approach the queen in her love (*furentem*)? How could he possibly begin?" (283–4). This is the crisis, and these are the questions that concern him, as he casts his mind back and forth in heroic thought (285–6), and they are very human questions indeed. This is no unfeeling automaton. What is easy to do is resolved upon and quickly carried out. He summons "Mnestheus, Sergestus, and brave Serestus," ordering them to convene the men and prepare the ships quietly, on some pretext or other. He himself, he says, will find some way to tell Dido, who, unaware, cannot expect that such love is at an end. All joyfully carry out his orders (288–95).

Virgil doesn't tell us directly what we soon find out, that Aeneas is the only one who doesn't carry out his assignment. Dido, fearful and percipient in her love, hears of the Trojan preparations and understands what they mean. It is she who approaches Aeneas, in fury and despair, in the great scene that follows, but we will leave it there.

The dominating presence in this scene, then, is the Roman hero, forced suddenly to recover his sense of mission. Again, we should not look for dramatic motivation here, asking how Aeneas could so instantaneously and unquestioningly resume his mission, just as we should not concern ourselves with whether he was "right" to fall in love with Dido in the first place or was morally "wrong" to abandon her so easily now. Virgil was clearly not concerned with such questions. The very abruptness, the inhuman harshness of his immediate assent to divine command is what Virgil gives us, and it is more a comment on the workings of divine order than on human behavior.

It is easy to miss entirely, or to downplay, what Virgil can bring out only indirectly, and that is that Aeneas cannot express the emotions that he will gradually be revealed to have. He does not go to Dido, as he said he would, because there are no words to express to her what he feels, since the action that has been forced upon him would show his words to be false. Simply, how can he say, "I love you," and then immediately leave her? Or how can he explain to her that he must continue now with the heroic mission, and then claim to love her still? This is the very crisis, the moment of human indecision, that Virgil forces on his hero, and it is much like the crises of our two previous scenes in its tension, its pull of opposites, in that the human response cannot be the response of the hero.

So Dido must come to him, as she does in the next scene, with words of anger and grief. He can offer her only a legalistic brief, making his case like a lawyer, as he himself says (*'pro re pauca loquar'* is legal language, 337).

There is no sense of his own regret or of his love. His speech is like that of
the shade of Creusa (2.776–89) or that of the image of Anchises (5.724–39),
both of whom have become the messengers of the divine order, the
spokespersons for the mission. But just as they can manage nevertheless
to remind Aeneas of their former human love, so Aeneas allows himself, at
the end of his official text, four words of what he really feels, "It is not my
will to go to Italy" ('*Italiam non sponte sequor*', 4.361).

The Hero and Personal Loss

Dido (4.331–61)

It is a wonder that there have been so many readers who have failed to
see, much less share, Aeneas' anguish at leaving Dido and his grief at her
death. But even stranger is that there have been many – and there still
are – who have seen Dido only as the wicked seductress, the enemy of
Rome.

It is understandable, though, that one's first reaction to Book IV would
be an utter condemnation of the Roman hero for his callow insensitivity
and complete inhuman disregard for the woman he had supposedly felt
real love for. It could hardly be otherwise, when Virgil's main purpose was
to show precisely the crushing force of Roman destiny and to cast his hero
according to the pattern of Apollonius' Jason and Catullus' Theseus. It is
easy to miss the finer strokes.

'*Italiam non sponte sequor*' ("Not of my own will do I go to Italy"): as we
have just seen, this is the only personal note in Aeneas' legalistic speech
to Dido, but it rings true. We may be sure of this by noting the formulaic
transition from Dido's tirade to Aeneas' response: "She had spoken. But he,
at Jupiter's command, held his gaze fixed and with effort suppressed his
love deep in his heart" (331–2). He cannot speak of his love (*curam*),
cannot show it or allow it to affect his purpose. Virgil, though, makes sure
that we see it. Dido answers in the third of this triad of speeches, collapses,
and is carried off by her attendants. "But pious [!] Aeneas, though wanting
to soothe her grief and anguish by words [!] of comfort, with many groans,
shaken in his soul with his great love for her, nevertheless obeys the divine
commands and returns to the fleet" (. . . *multa gemens magnoque animum
labefactus amore* . . . , 393–6). Nothing could be clearer, or more moving.
The Roman hero remains unmoved, but his human suffering is there
to see.

Aeneas is permitted his grief only when it is too late, when in the Underworld Dido, in her turn unspeaking and unmoved, turns away from him.

"The Trojan hero" (*Troius heros*, 6.451) sees her, an indistinct shadow among the shades, like a new moon barely seen through a mist, and with tears he speaks to her at last with his full love. He swears again that it was not his wish to leave her (*'invitus, regina, tuo de litore cessi'*, 460 – a strange, almost verbatim use of a line of Catullus), but divine command (he repeats) drove him. It is then that she turns away, leaving him to his inadequate words and tears (*talibus Aeneas ardentem et torva tuentem / lenibat dictis animum lacrimasque ciebat*, 467–8), and returns to the mutual love of Sychaeus.

Creusa (2.775–95)

Aeneas and his family begin their flight from Troy. He takes his father on his shoulders and his son by the hand. "Let the boy Iulus accompany me, and let my wife follow at a distance (*longe*)" (2.710–11). Why "at a distance"? It makes no sense. From antiquity until now answers have been proposed, all inadequate and most silly, trying to explain away or excuse something that Virgil felt no need to apologize for. He was not interested in the "why?" or whether Aeneas acted stupidly, with reprehensible lack of concern for his wife. He was interested only in the fact, that something inexplicable and terrible did happen, and this single adverb, "at a distance," coming from his own mouth, is our first shock of the reality that is to come.

As they proceed through the dark streets and are almost at the gates, there is a sudden alarm: the sound and flash of Greek arms, panic, and flight, and Creusa is lost in the confusion. That is what happened, for no reason. The first step of the Roman mission involved the senseless loss of the hero's dear wife. Aeneas himself is relating these events to Dido and her guests, and he asks, "Whom of gods and men did I not accuse in my madness, or *what thing more cruel did I see in the fall of my city*?" (745–6).

Aeneas returns to their home and to the center of the city in his vain search for her. In his frenzy of despair she appears, or rather her likeness (*simulacrum*), her ghost (*umbra*), an image larger than life (*et nota maior imago*, 772–3). She speaks to him, though, as we have noted, only as the voice of Roman destiny, telling him, on divine command, of the journey in exile to Italy, where there will be a new kingdom and a royal wife. Only at the beginning and end of her speech does she allow herself, a wife and mother, a word of human sorrow and compassion. Her first words tell Aeneas not to indulge his senseless grief, but she adds, "my dear husband" (*'o dulcis coniunx'*, 776–7). And her final farewell is a plea to remember the love of their common son (*'iamque vale et nati serva communis amorem'*, 789).

With these words she leaves him and "disappears into thin air" (*tenuisque recessit in auras*, 791), just as Eurydice had left Orpheus on the threshold of the upper world, "like smoke dispersed into thin air" (*ceu fumus in auras / commixtus tenuis, Geo.* 4.499–500), and just as Anchises' apparition in Sicily left Aeneas (*et tenuis fugit ceu fumus in auras*, 5.740). "Three times I tried to embrace her," says Aeneas, "and three times her image escaped my vain grasp, like insubstantial air, like a fleeting dream" (2.792–4) – three lines that are repeated exactly when Aeneas tries to embrace the shade of his father in the Underworld (6.700–2).

For a moment let us return to our initial question – why does Aeneas specifically tell Creusa to follow him "at a distance" (*longe*)? As the verbal echoes just mentioned show, Orpheus' Eurydice was the first of Virgil's figures of senseless loss, and Virgil had her in mind when thinking of Creusa. Both Eurydice and Creusa were lost at a final moment, when escape seemed assured (*iam luce sub ipsa, Geo.* 4.490; *iamque propinquabam portis omnemque videbar / evasisse viam*, 2.730–1). Eurydice quite naturally was following Orpheus, and so then does Creusa follow Aeneas, and of both of them the same archaic adverb *pone* is used (= *post*, "behind": *pone sequens, Geo.* 4.487; *pone subit coniunx*, 2.725 – *pone* occurs only twice elsewhere in Virgil). Both leave their husbands with words yet unspoken (. . . *et multa volentem / dicere, Geo.* 4.501–2 = *Aen.* 2.790–1). As Eurydice and Creusa became almost one in Virgil's mind, *longe*, "at a distance," would seem to have been, perhaps not logical, but inevitable.

Anchises (6.679–702)

Almost all of the poetry of Catullus is in one way or another concerned with loss and betrayal, to such an extent that he would seem to have written from intense personal experience over a short period of time. His longer poems are the highly stylized, poetic abstractions of the emotional reality of the shorter poems. The two central experiences of his life were the loss of his brother, who died (we must guess) while serving on the governor's staff in Bithynia (hence Troy, for Catullus), and his betrayal by Lesbia. In his abstractions of these experiences, the two themes merge; thus, for instance, Ariadne in poem 64 suffers the loss of home, her family, and all that is dear because of her betrayal by Theseus, the foreign hero. Love leads only to her abandonment on a barren shore.

Catullus, we know, went to Bithynia for a year on Memmius' staff. One purpose, if not the main one, of this most uncongenial exile was to pay his brother the last rites of burial. The 10 lines of poem 101 are the perfect distillation of this experience. It begins,

Having sailed through many peoples, through many seas,
 I come, brother, to these unhappy last rites,
To offer you this final duty, my gift, in death
 And to speak with you, now but ash, silent, in vain.

*Multas per gentes et multa per aequora vectus
 advenio has miseras, frater, ad inferias,
ut te postremo donarem munere mortis
 et mutam nequiquam alloquerer cinerem.*

And it ends with the ritual words, "and forever, brother, hail and farewell" (*atque in perpetuum, frater, ave atque vale*). Even after such a journey, no communication was possible.

Variations of the first line of poem 101 recur in the first books of the *Aeneid* as a sort of *Leitmotif* for Aeneas' wanderings, but even so we are not prepared to hear Anchises, in the Underworld, greet his son, "I receive you, [you who have] sailed through what lands, through how many seas" (*'quas ego te terras et quanta per aequora vectum / accipio'*, 6.692–3). Human contact with the dead is indeed possible, it seems: what Catullus could not do, Aeneas has accomplished. His *pietas* has indeed overcome the impossible journey, as Anchises has just said (*'venisti tandem, tuaque exspectata parenti / vicit iter durum pietas'*, 687–8), and words *can* be exchanged between the living and the dead (*'datur ora tueri, / nate, tua et notas audire et reddere voces'*, 688–9 – there is no way of knowing for certain whether Virgil intended this as a statement or a question). Aeneas replies that it was his father's frequent apparition (*'tua tristis imago'*, 695) that brought him here. He reaches out to his father: "Give me your hand, father, and don't withdraw from my embrace" (*'da iungere dextram, / da, genitor, teque amplexu ne subtrahe nostro'*, 697–8). But he finds that it is only an image. "Three times then he tried to embrace him, and three times the image escaped his vain grasp, like the insubstantial air, like a fleeting dream" (700–2), lines repeated verbatim from Book II, as he tried to embrace Creusa's ghost.

We return for a moment to the apparition in Sicily, with its suggestions of Eurydice and Creusa, to Aeneas' anguished words as his father's image fades "like smoke into thin air": "Where then do you rush off to? From whom do you flee? Who keeps you from my embrace?" (5.741–2). The Catullan finality of death is affirmed.

Venus (1.305–410)

Aeneas is denied all human contact – with Dido after his forced resumption of the role of Roman hero, and with his wife Creusa and father

Anchises when, after death, they become the spokespersons for the Roman mission. Again and again in these scenes we see him reaching out in desperation to those he loves, all in vain. He is a hero in a terrible isolation.

What of his mother? When we see her first, in Book I, she has gone to Jupiter out of concern for her son, shipwrecked on a hostile coast after seven years of wandering. The scene is patterned on one in the first book of the *Iliad*, when Achilles, deprived of Briseis and dishonored by Agamemnon, is comforted by his mother Thetis as he weeps on the shore at Troy: she listens to him with all the warmth and sympathy of a human mother and then makes her appeal directly to Zeus. Venus, however, has gone to Jupiter without offering any comfort to her son, and in fact her whole, somewhat querulous, request to the father of gods and men (1.229–53) shows little if any concern for Aeneas' suffering and despair. Her exclusive concern is for the promise of Roman destiny, and her son is but the means to her own future glory. Jupiter seems to recognize this immediately and with amusement, and his response is entirely about the Rome to come.

Encouraged that what has been ordained remains unshaken, Venus then goes to Libya, not to offer sympathy or understanding to a son, but to see to it that the next small steps toward destiny will be successfully managed. She finds Aeneas and faithful Achates exploring the unknown territory. In a scene that is almost comic, instead of encouraging her son directly, as had Thetis, she assumes the dress and appearance of a traditional huntress-devotee of Diana, "like some Spartan girl, or like Thracian Harpalyce" (315–17). Though Aeneas feels some unease about the identity of this apparition, his mother persists and takes the opportunity to relate Dido's history (335–70). "And who are you?" she asks in concluding. Aeneas' answer shows him to be in total despair ("A stranger in dire want, I wander the wastes of Libya, driven from Europe and Asia," 384–5), but his mother cuts him off "in the middle of his grief, not allowing further complaint" (385–6). After a bit of staged augury, she tells him, simply, to get on with it (*'perge modo et, qua te ducit via, derige gressum'*, 401).

"She spoke, and turning away" revealed herself as truly a goddess. It is a terrible thing, in this epic, to have a goddess for a mother, and when Aeneas recognizes "his mother, fleeing from him" (*ille ubi matrem / agnovit ... fugientem*, 405–6), he reacts with anger: "Why so often do you, too, deceive and mock your son so cruelly with false images? Why is it not granted to join hands, to hear and return real words in human conversation?" (*'quid natum totiens, crudelis tu quoque, falsis / ludis imaginibus? Cur dextrae iungere dextram / non datur ac veras audire et reddere voces?'*, 407–9).

When Thetis heard her son calling in tears to her in the depths of the sea, "quickly she rose like a mist on the grey sea and sat down by him as he wept, stroked his hand, spoke a word, and called him by name" (*Il.* 1.359–61): Homer's formulaic language powerfully conveys the essence of maternal love and sympathy. Virgil, in an intended contrast, show us a mother revealed only when she turns from her son and flees. There is no touch, no real words, only these images and deceptions, like the image of his father in the Underworld, when it seemed for a delusive moment that human contact even with the dead might be possible (*'datur ora tueri, / nate, tua et notas audire et reddere voces'*, 6.688–9).

One small word, though, should not be overlooked, and that is *quoque*, "also", in the phrase *'crudelis tu quoque'* ("you, too, cruel"). It is a phrase that goes back to the *Eclogues*, used there of Venus in a telling context (*Ecl.* 8.48), and thereby carrying real Virgilian weight here. "You also cruel," but who are the others, we want to ask. Virgil's web of verbal associations, the threads that we have just been gathering, clearly involve Eurydice, Creusa, Dido, and Anchises. To be the hero of Virgil's Roman epic is to suffer personal loss, again and again, and to do so is to be left alone, abandoned.

Ascanius (12.432–40)

What, finally, of his son?

Ascanius is the Roman future, as Virgil often reminds us, and we need only to call him by his other name, Iulus, to know this. Does this, then, explain what has often been observed, that this father and son have such a distant relationship in a poem where other parents and children are exemplars of parental-filial closeness?

Aeneas speaks directly to his son only once in the entire poem, in the final book, after his wound has been cured and he has armed himself for battle (12.432–40). He embraces his son and kisses him – "through his helmet" (*summaque per galeam delibans oscula*, 434). It would be impossible for the Roman reader not to think immediately of Hector's final embrace of his infant son, when he took off the helmet that had just so frightened the boy and then, placing it on the ground, kissed him (*Il.* 6.466–74). Hector then speaks to his son, with a prayer to Zeus and the other gods that Astyanax will become a better warrior than his father and rule at Troy, and that he delight his mother, bringing back to her the bloody spoils of an enemy killed in battle. This is, sadly, all he can say or pray for, but by the end of the *Aeneid* we can hope for something better from Aeneas, some expression of the futility of all the killing, some wish for peace. We do not get it: "Learn, my son, from me, what it is to be a hero, and the meaning of struggle – from others, good fortune" (*'disce, puer, virtutem ex me verumque laborem, / fortunam ex aliis'*, 435–6). And when Ascanius has become a man, "May your father Aeneas and your uncle Hector stir you as you contemplate the deeds of your people" (439–40, repeating the words of Andromache, 3.343). Has Aeneas no other message for his son than to continue on the way of the heroic ideal, after all that he himself has suffered and after all the destruction and death that the old way, *virtus*, has caused?

The Hero as Warrior (10.510–605)

Though the *Iliad* may seem to many first-time readers to contain endless stretches of indiscriminate slaughter, there are organizing principles at work, deriving from the earliest traditions of oral poetry. One of these principles, which must go back to the bard's song recounting the exploits of his lord and patron, is the *aristeia*, the account of the hero at his best, on a day when everything goes his way and he can do no wrong; he seems to be filled with a spirit for battle which is greater than human, and often indeed a god appears at his side.

The most notable is the *aristeia* of Achilles in Books XX–XXI. Patroclus' death has produced in Achilles a fury that is close to madness, to the pure destructiveness of fire. No one can stand against him (both Aeneas and Hector need to be rescued by divine intervention), and as he cuts his way through the Trojan ranks to the banks of the Xanthus River, his progress is repeatedly compared to raging fire. He ultimately comes face to face with the personified river, and then, with what can only be called surrealism, it is no longer Achilles but Hephaestus who faces the Xanthus, until the river begins to boil like a cauldron. Achilles' *aristeia* is transformed into the elemental opposition of fire and water, with fire ultimately the victor.

Virgil's fascination with this scene is evident in the opening section of the *Georgics* and throughout; the whole poem, indeed, returns again and again to the opposition of fire and water, the destructiveness of war opposed to civilizing progress. Book X of the *Aeneid* is the centerpiece of Homeric battle. It begins with Aeneas' return with the fleet; then the *aristeia* of Pallas and his death at the hands of Turnus; then Aeneas' *aristeia*; and finally the deaths of Lausus and Mezentius at the hands of Aeneas. The 100 lines of Aeneas' *aristeia* are thus central to (and almost the center of) Virgil's own miniature *Iliad* and reveal another aspect of the hero. What sort of hero is this?

We need to begin briefly with Aeneas' landing (10.260–75). In a different context we will look further into the pattern Aeneas here provides for Octavian at Actium. Our main impression is of the fire that blazes from Aeneas' head, helmet, and shield, like bloody comets banefully glowing red in a clear sky, or like Sirius, the dog star of summer, bringing thirst and fever to wretched mortals. The vast flames poured forth from Aeneas' arms are the destructive fire of Achilles' *aristeia*, for the simile comes directly from the *Iliad*, when Priam at the beginning of Book XXII sees the gleam of Achilles' bronze, like the fire of Orion's dog (i.e., Sirius), "which is the brightest, made to be a baneful sign, and brings much fever-heat to wretched mortals" (*Il.* 22.25–32).

Word comes to Aeneas of Pallas' death (510–12). Pallas, Evander, their hospitality and pledges "are all before his eyes" as he begins ("all aflame," *ardens*) the slaughter. First, he captures alive eight Rutulians to be sacrificed at Pallas' funeral (and Virgil does not forget about them – they are sent off to Pallanteum in the funeral procession, 11.81–2), just as Achilles took twelve victims to be sacrificed at Patroclus' funeral (*Il.* 21.27–32). There is no way to gloss over the fact of human sacrifice in Virgil's poem.

His next victim is Magus, who is an exact counterpart to Lycaon, a son of Priam, the next victim of Achilles. Lycaon had been captured by Achilles before, had been sold, and had just returned to Troy to fight again; he begs for mercy, but this time Achilles refuses – the time for ransom was before Patroclus had been killed, "but now, friend, die, you too" (21.99–106). Magus falls to Aeneas' knees and begins his supplication with an appeal to both Anchises and Iulus: "Through your father's shades and the future of rising Iulus, I beseech you, spare my life for my son and my father" (524–5). He then offers ransom money; Aeneas scorns the money on grounds similar to Achilles' rejection, as we might expect, but we would not have expected his final taunt: "Let the shades of my father Anchises, let Iulus see this thrust."

Next he kills a priest of Apollo and Diana (537–42), wearing a sacred fillet and clothed in gleaming white, but the killing is in fact a sacrifice (*immolat*), and Mars (not Apollo or Diana) receives the priest's arms as a trophy.

Aeneas' rage continues (*Dardanides contra furit*, 545). He kills a certain Tarquitus (550–60), the son of sylvan Faunus and Dryope, suggestive of natural innocence. He too pleads for his life, in vain, for Aeneas beheads him, even as he pleads, and taunts the headless trunk: "Now lie there, you who were to be feared. Your fine mother will not give you burial and lay your body in your ancestral tomb. You will be left to the wild birds, or the waves will carry you sunk in the flood, and hungry fish will lick your wounds." These are the words of Achilles to Lycaon (21.122–8), but Aeneas' blatant savagery cannot be excused or explained away on the grounds that Virgil was simply following a Homeric model. Is it so hard to accept that Virgil put into his poem only what he wanted to be there?

What Virgil has put next, too, is not easily explained away. Aeneas is compared to the hundred-handed giant Aegaeon, also called Briareus, under which name he appears as one of the monsters at the entrance to the Underworld (6.287). In the simile here Aegaeon belches fire from his fifty mouths and breasts, fighting against Jupiter (10.565–70), and "thus did Aeneas rage (*desaevit*) over the whole field, victorious, when once his blade grew warm." The giants, in their attack on Jupiter, are always, without exception, representative of blind and brute violence against rationality and order, in both art and literature. Virgil could not have meant otherwise. But this is "the Trojan hero" (*Troius heros*, 584), our "pious Aeneas" (*pius Aeneas*, 591), who now kills two brothers, taunting them for their fraternal bond (575–601).

"Such slaughter did the Dardanian leader wreak through the field, raging like a torrent in flood or a black whirlwind" (*talia per campos edebat funera ductor / Dardanius torrentis aquae vel turbinis atri / more furens*, 602–4). So ends the *aristeia* of Aeneas.

Some Observations on Character

Aeneas' rage began with the death of Pallas, and it ended, just as abruptly, with his killing of Lausus.

Lausus' attempt to shield his wounded father Mezentius from Aeneas' fury is a paradigm of *pietas*, as is scornfully recognized by Aeneas himself. "Why do you rush headlong to death and dare deeds greater than your strength? Your piety deceives you, careless" (10.811–12), he taunts, no less maddened (*demens*) and driven by savage anger (*saevae irae*). He strikes at Lausus with his sword, and the blade penetrates not only shield and armor, but even "the tunic which his mother had woven with delicate gold" (818).

The sight of Lausus at the moment of death suddenly restores "the son of Anchises" (*Anchisiades*, 822) to his senses. He groans in pity, reaches forth his hand, and "the image of filial piety occurred to him" (*et mentem patriae subiit pietatis imago*, 824). He grants the boy his armor and burial in his ancestral tomb.

What, exactly, has happened here? Aeneas' *aristeia* is a study in *pietas* totally inverted, not just gone wrong but turned completely upside down, or inside out. How can the hero, whose predominant heroic quality is *pietas*, suddenly turn to acts of savage impiety, reminding us of Neoptolemus' slaughter of Priam at the altar, or of the hero's final act in the poem, when "fired by madness and terrible in his anger" he suddenly drives his sword into Turnus? And how are we to understand the transformation of

Mezentius, the paragon of all evil, who dies here at the end of Book X with tragic and heroic dignity, thoroughly sympathetic? And what finally do we make of heroism itself in this poem, whether the heroic ideal of Homer or the national glory of future Rome? Ultimately, what does Virgil mean when the ideals of *virtus* and *pietas* so often seem to lead to or become their opposites? Before going on to explore these questions in greater detail, it will be helpful to sketch out some general concepts that Virgil and his readers took for granted – the instinctive ways they thought about character.

Character and behavior

"Character" is one of those things that we accept, at any one time, without much thought or questioning. I know what you mean when you say, "John is a good boy," and you know what I mean when I say, "It's such a shame about Jane – she had so much promise when she was young, but she certainly took a wrong turn somewhere along the way." We assume, you and I, that John might eventually go on to defraud his company of millions, and that Jane, with some help at the right moment, might have been saved from her sad end. We easily assume that good people can go wrong and that the bad can be saved by some intervention or experience: that is, that character can change. Or – if we begin to think about it – perhaps not? Might there not always have been some stain of "evil" in John which we just couldn't see? Doesn't Freudian psychology (say) find that our earliest experience so dominates our lives that any change is superficial?

It has become a commonplace among classical scholars that both the Greeks and the Romans viewed the character of an individual as something fixed at birth, unchanging throughout life. This would be the basic assumption of any Roman you met on the street – that is, this is what would be in his mind if you began a conversation with him about the character of the emperor Tiberius, though of course, as the conversation proceeded, he would be perfectly able to view Tiberius in a number of other ways. *Ingenium* is the usual word for "character," that which is "inborn," related to *genius* and a number of other words, such as *natura*, from the same root. But it is obvious that people behave in very different ways at different times and in different circumstances. A distinction, then, is assumed between character (something fixed) and behavior (what appears to change). One common word for behavior is *mores*, the totality of an individual's "ways" or "habits," which is too often translated as "character." The distinction between character and behavior is always worth keeping in mind when reading ancient biography or whenever an ancient writer offers an assessment of an individual: how does Sallust, for example, understand Catiline, or Tacitus conceive of Tiberius' career? And since cities too had their own characters, what do Roman historians, such as Livy, find fixed in Rome's character, and what external influences caused changes in its historical behavior?

Change in behavior is generally the result of change in external circumstances. Certain restraints, for instance, can be removed or can cease to be effective, as, for instance, with the death of a parent or the end of the influence of a teacher, which then allows the true character of an individual greater expression or freer play, until perhaps eventually all restraining influences have been removed and one's real character is revealed. There is a fascinating example of this sort of thinking in Plautus' *Mostellaria*, in the first song of the playboy Philolaches (84–156), who compares, at length, the character of a man to the building of a house and the outside influences, from its builders to its subsequent owners, that work upon it. In his own case, he sings, as long as he was under the control of others, he was fine, but "after I came into to my own character (*immigravi ingenium in meum*), all the work of the builders went for naught, right away and completely" (135–6), and then came a succession of bad behaviors, from indolence to love. It is not often that we can find Romans talking about such things so clearly, because our common assumptions and self-evident attitudes don't require detailed exposition. This view of character is something almost reflexive, unthinking, but it can often be seen as an underlying assumption (as it is, for example, consistently in Tacitus' presentation of the Julio-Claudians). For instance, what might we need to assume as the basic character (*ingenium*) of Camilla, as her environment changes from the rustic and pastoral to the military (an easy progression, from huntress to warrior) and her final attraction to purple and gold?

But Aeneas does not develop and change in the course of Virgil's narrative (though many readers have seen a development). This is not a poem about a hero who learns at each stage of his journey and who finally emerges triumphant at the end, having discovered his identity. To understand him better we need to consider another, less commonly recognized, Roman view of character.

Character as balance

The earliest Greek medical writings went under the name of the Coan physician Hippocrates, though they are clearly the work of different hands over a period of time, as a rational understanding of man and his world was developing in Ionian cities in the fifth century BC. Several of the early treatises, such as *Airs, Waters, Places*, offer a systematic view not just of an individual's health and sickness, but of the character of separate peoples based on the situation of their land, seasonal changes, and climate. A system of oppositions develops, and in a short time the list of opposites is reduced to the four elements (earth, air, fire, and water) with their four qualities (cold, dry, hot, and wet) and (eventually) their corresponding humors (moistures) in the human body (blood, phlegm, yellow and black bile). So much could be done with these oppositions, and so much of our universe could be explained through them, that they remained dominant in the European mind until modern science and medicine.

Everything in the physical world is composed of the four elements, which, mixed in different proportions, produce different materials. Some rocks, therefore, are harder than others, and some woods burn more easily or are less subject to rot, because of the different mixture of the elements they contain. Mixture is crucial in everything, but the ideal mixture of any one thing is continually subject to being upset. This can happen, for instance, when seasons change, when, in the spring, the cold and wet (phlegm, in the body) of winter is changing to the hot and dry (yellow bile) of summer, upsetting the balances of the humors in our bodies and producing sicknesses, often due to an excess of blood (hot and wet) that is the result of the natural balance of spring. There is an elegant simplicity to the theory of the elements which can be applied to every aspect of our world – from the physical sciences to the microcosm of man. With this system we can understand not just man's health and physical nature (that is, the differences, for instance, between the sexes, or the changes in the body through the different stages of human life), but social differences too (ethnography) and even human psychology.

We are all familiar with the modern European manifestations of the four humors – the sanguine character, the phlegmatic, choleric, and melancholic. The system has become rigid and enclosed. In antiquity it was much less so, but at the same time it was so pervasive and accepted in the popular mind that it passed without comment or special notice. No writer sits down to describe and define what everybody instinctively knows, but rather to set out and discuss what is novel, original, and different. Thus, for example, the four Stoic emotions (fear, desire, grief, and joy – so in *Aeneid* 6.733, *hinc metuunt cupiuntque, dolent gaudentque*) appear to be different from the four humoral characters. My purpose is not to reduce Virgil to any system (he never so limited himself), but rather to bring out a way of thinking about character that was an intellectual given, for him and his readers, but may not be so apparent to us.

In the healthy body its constituent humors (elements) are in perfect balance, perfectly mixed. When the mixture is thrown out of balance, the body becomes sick, and this is usually the result of an imbalance in the environment – for example, a wet summer (instead of the usual dry) with exceptional heat. Germs, of course, were unknown, and therefore there was no clear concept of an external, invasive cause of sickness. It was possible, then, to think of health and sickness not as opposite states, but simply as an altered mixture of the same elements within the body. This is a simple concept, but hard to grasp, since it is not at all the way we tend to think.

"Why am I sick today?" I might ask, and I would answer, "Because I caught a virus, which invaded my body, something bad that must be driven out if I am to feel better." A Roman might answer the question, "Because, due to this month's unusual weather, I have an imbalance in my body that produces these opposites within me, fever and chills." We tend, therefore, to see sickness (bad) and health (good) as a polarity. For a Roman, the body (or, we might say, character, *ingenium*) in health and in sickness is the same body (character), composed of the same four elements, qualities, humors; sickness and health (behaviors) are of course different states, but the polarities are those of the elements within, the hot opposed to the cold, the wet to the dry, always changing their balance and mixture in response to changes in the environment. It is the same stream, whether it stands frozen in the winter, or rages in flood over its banks in the spring, or runs cool and refreshing in the heat of the summer.

We can finally get back to Aeneas. Is he good or bad? Is he cold, wooden, and even inhuman (when for instance he leaves Dido), or is he thoroughly human (as when he reaches continually for the human contact that is always denied to him)? Is he a paragon of the heroic ideal, advancing it toward the grandeur of the new world order, or is he the exemplar of the savagery and brutality of war? All such questions are the result of our thinking in polarities, and even when we try to find a compromise (by saying, for instance, that Virgil might sometimes "undercut" or cast doubt upon an Augustan ideal), we still think, basically, of Good versus Bad.

Now I am certainly not saying that the Romans did not have such simple oppositions or were not given to, or capable of, thinking in polarities, because they could think in such terms just as easily as we do, and Virgil so often gives us the black and white of their preconceptions. But I am saying that there was another way of thought, common and instinctive, that we do not easily recognize. A Roman did not have to see, or settle for, a good Aeneas or a bad, but was able to see one man, made of the same constituent passions, which, when in balance, produced a healthy state, but when unbalanced, a state of disease.

We can see these ideas throughout the *Georgics*, where Virgil rings the changes upon them continually, in wonderful ways, and we will try to outline these ideas in a later chapter, as background for the *Aeneid*. Virgil's epic focuses on *virtus* and *pietas*, and we can all agree on the excellence of these ideals. But Virgil can show us the martial fire of heroism totally out of balance, resulting in savagery, or the *pietas* of the Roman hero resulting in Dido's death. The actors in Virgil's epic – the human actors, at least – are in themselves neither good nor bad, just as my body, when I wake up one morning with the flu, is the same one I had when I went to bed feeling fine. Aeneas at the end of the poem, acting from madness and anger, is the very same hero whom we first meet, wishing that he had fallen at Troy.

2

The Victims

Virgil's hero exists in an impersonal isolation, stripped of every human contact and facing a future that seems to offer none. All those whom he meets throughout the epic suffer as well. The progress toward Rome, in human terms, is not a happy one.

It is not hard to see what it is that destroys so many, or what the victims have in common, but it is another aspect of the poem that has sometimes been ignored or misrepresented. The future of the Roman order (as has been thought) may have demanded sacrifice, and much stood in its way that had to be eliminated if right and justice were eventually to prevail: these are premises that some may want to accept. But were the victims really obstacles to progress, and were they necessary sacrifices?

Dido

A widowed queen and a teenage girl: it may seem strange that, when Aeneas and Dido first meet, there are clear suggestions of the meeting of Odysseus and Nausicaa in *Odyssey* VI. For example, Virgil's simile comparing Dido to Diana among her Oreads (1.498–504) is a direct replay of Homer's simile comparing Nausicaa to Artemis among her nymphs (*Od.* 6.102–9), and Aeneas, just before emerging from his cloud, is given supernatural beauty by Venus, like a work of ivory or of silver and gold (1.589–93), just as Athene had made Odysseus resplendent, like a work of gold and silver (*Od.* 6.229–35). We are made to remember as well Apollonius' Medea and her immediate infatuation with Jason. But both Nausicaa and Medea are young girls for whom love is a new experience, whereas Dido is a queen, founding her own city, and a widow.

With these allusions, though, Virgil has turned the Carthaginian queen, the historical enemy of Rome and a precedent for Cleopatra, into a very different figure: Dido will become a composite of Nausicaa, Medea, and Catullus' Ariadne, betrayed and abandoned by the hero, as we have already had occasion to see.

We see Dido for the first time just as Aeneas does, as she and her entourage enter the temple of Juno, where he has been gazing, in deep sadness, at the scenes of the war at Troy. Dido is very much the queen: seated amidst her guard, she is the law-giver and founder of her city (1.507–8), and the Trojan Ilioneus, when he enters, addresses her as such: "O queen, to whom Jupiter has granted to found a new city with justice and to restrain arrogant peoples" (522–3) – her role here seems very much, in fact, like Rome's divine mission. The whole scene is a calculated exaggeration of epic grandeur, with its two sets of paired speeches, with the entrance first of Ilioneus and his men from the seven lost ships and then Aeneas' dramatic emergence from the cloud (which nobody in the temple had noticed?), divinely refulgent, and with the two choruses of Carthaginians and Trojans – nothing could be more operatic. They all leave the temple for the palace, where a banquet is prepared with settings of purple, gold, and silver, reliefs on the plate showing "the heroic deeds of ancestors, a long series of events stretching through so many generations of heroes from the ancient origin of the people" (639–42).

Among the many extraordinary details of this grand and momentous meeting, two discordant notes are to be heard. The first, as we have just observed, are the allusions to Odysseus and Nausicaa, which inevitably bring to our minds Medea and Ariadne and heroic betrayal. The second sounds in Aeneas' own concluding words to Dido: "So long as rivers run down to the sea, so long as shadows play over the hollows on mountain sides, so long as stars pasture on the pole of heaven, always will your honor, name, and praise be with me, wherever I go" (1.607–9). The trope is erotic, unmistakably.

As the queen drinks deep of love during the banquet of the first night, it is clear that she has been captivated by the heroism of Aeneas. She questions Aeneas insistently about Priam, Hector, the arms of Memnon, the horses of Diomedes, and great Achilles (748–52), and Aeneas responds with his complete account of the fall of Troy and his wanderings, a miniature *Iliad* and *Odyssey* (Books II and III).

The five lines that resume the narrative at the beginning of Book IV are among the richest in Virgil's poem. The controlling images of fire and wound are set forth etymologically (1–2) and developed (3–5). It is the *viri virtus*, "the heroic qualities of the hero," his Homeric lineage (*gentis honos*), and his appearance and speech (*vultus verbaque*) that are like shafts wounding her heart. Her love allows her no rest (note *cura, recursat*, and *cura* at the ends of lines 1, 3, and 5): the ancient etymology of *cura* as *quod cor urit* ("because it burns the heart") can be traced back before Virgil and was well known.

When Dido speaks of her passion to her sister Anna (9–29), it is again clear that she is a victim, initially at least, of the fatal attraction of heroism. "Who is this stranger?" she asks. "How noble in appearance, how strong! He is descended, clearly, from the gods, for fear convicts spirits of baseness, and what battles he has told of" (10–14). She is like a doe wounded by a shepherd unaware (in the wonderful simile of lines 68–73), and the fire and the wound do their work, but it is again the hero's words and deeds that cause the wounds: "and repeatedly at day's end, mad with love, she asks to hear of the struggles at Troy, and repeatedly she hangs on Aeneas' every word" (77–9). And as love consumes her, she ceases to be the queen, abandoning the direction of building operations and military training (86–9). In less than 100 lines Virgil has shown us, has made us feel through language and image, Dido's progress from the grand queen, ruler of her people and founder of what will become a great city, to a lover in the isolation of her madness.

Just as her passion was caused by this visitor from the heroic world (as Virgil stresses repeatedly), so the inevitable result is brought about by Aeneas' sudden departure, with no explanation offered by either Aeneas or Virgil other than Jupiter's commands. We have looked into this previously, but it is worth noting again just what Virgil is concerned with, and what he isn't. His exploration and presentation of Dido's madness and suicide are a marvel for which there are no words, both terrifying and evocative of our deepest sympathy. But of Aeneas' human emotions there is nothing, or almost nothing, so that we may not even notice, until we look a second time, that this is Virgil's whole point – that the anguish felt by Dido's lover has to be suppressed and cannot be uttered to her or even admitted to himself, as the epic's hero, "groaning deeply, shaken in his soul with his great love, nevertheless follows the divine commands and returns to his fleet" (395–6). Virgil's story of Dido is that of the impersonal heroic world that meets, fascinates, and finally consumes and destroys an individual deceived and abandoned, but this hero (unlike Apollonius' Jason and Catullus' Theseus) is deeply affected as well.

There it is. Yet again Virgil's poetry has been reduced to a simple message, totally inadequate. But it may serve as a starting point, a perspective from which a reader can follow the story again, unencumbered by such irrelevant questions as whether Aeneas was right or wrong, or whether Dido should or should not have betrayed her sense of *pudor* (whatever that might be) for Sychaeus and allowed herself to fall in love.

Much else, too, that concerned Virgil is there to see, such as the actual working out of the central images of fire and wound, the evolution of love into madness, and the realization of deception and betrayal.

There is one last observation to be made, though, before we leave Dido. The other major victims of the hero's progress in the poem, as we will see, are drawn into the heroic world, in one way or another, from outside, leaving their proper spheres because of the attraction of heroic glory, fame, or wealth. Dido, as we have just seen, was initially attracted by Aeneas' heroic qualities (deeds, words, lineage, and appearance), but she herself, as a queen, began as a part of that world. Instead of being drawn into it, she becomes farther and farther removed from it. The process, though, has been effectively completed near the beginning of Book IV (lines 86–9): what, then, is left for Virgil to do, after his queen has become a woman in love?

What he does is to follow Dido in her withdrawal, on and on into her private world of love and madness, where not even Anna is admitted. Terrified by what must come, she turns to suicide (450–1), observing all around her omens of death, seeing in her mad dreams Aeneas pursuing her fiercely; "she seems always to be left alone by herself, always to be going down a long road, seeking her Tyrians in a deserted land," driven mad (465–8). Aeneas (unwittingly, like the shepherd of the simile in lines 68–73) has taken her from her proper role as queen, from her people, and finally from her sister Anna, until her isolation at her death is complete, and terrible.

There is only one other character in the epic who suffers a similar progress to a similar isolation, cut off from every human contact, and that is Aeneas.

Nisus and Euryalus

Virgil tells the story of Nisus and Euryalus in three scenes. First, they are introduced as they stand on guard at night and realize the possibility of finding a way through the Rutulian lines to get word of the Trojans' dire situation to Aeneas, upriver at the site of Rome (9.176–223). Second, their proposal is approved by Iulus and the Trojan leaders (224–313). Third, the mission becomes a disaster (314–458). The whole episode takes place at night.

Virgil introduces them as unmistakable types (176–81). Nisus, the elder, had been sent by his mother to be a follower (*comitem*) of Aeneas. And who was she? A huntress by the name of Ida (her relation to the mountain is unclear), and her son is "swift of foot, with javelin and light arrows." This detail is not gratuitous: Nisus is another figure, like Camilla, who had belonged to the natural world (Ida?) where hunting had not yet become war. Euryalus is another type, the beautiful boy, the down of youth still on his cheek. Together they represent the classical ideal of love between man and boy, as Virgil had presented them in the foot race in Book V ("Euryalus distinguished for his beauty and youth, Nisus for his pious love of the boy" – *amore pio pueri*, 5.295–6). The episode is based on the night raid of Diomedes and Odysseus on the Trojan camp in Book X of the *Iliad*, with many of its details as well as its general outline taken over by Virgil. The epic tone, therefore, was set from the start, but Virgil's two characters are no Diomedes and Odysseus.

As the plan takes shape in Nisus' mind, erotic love is transformed into a thirst for heroic glory. "Do the gods," asks Nisus, "put passion (*ardorem*) into our minds, or does each one's raging desire (*dira cupido*) become his divinity?" (184–5) His mind, he continues, drives him now to battle, to some great deed, and is no longer content with calm and repose (*placida quiete*, 187) – that is, with the ideal state of the lover, traditionally opposed to the military life. Euryalus too is smitten with "a great love of heroic glory" (*magno laudum percussus amore*, 197) and demands to be included.

And so they take their plan to the leaders, meeting in formulaic council. Their reception is clearly intended to mark their transition into a new world, a passage to arms. Iulus promises a Homeric catalogue of gifts for their daring, almost a parody. The one note that is not Homeric, though, is the introduction of Euryalus' mother, whom, in the event of her son's death, Iulus, "struck by the image of filial piety," promises to care for – "she will be a mother to me, Creusa in all but name" (297–8). Heroism will shatter another human bond.

The mission itself is to find, quite literally, a *way* to Aeneas. So Nisus had first proposed to Euryalus (*viam*, 196), and so he had assured the council, "Nor does a way escape our notice" (*'nec nos via fallit euntis'*, 243), which we hear also as "Nor does the way deceive us." The first stage of the mission (314–66) is the actual making of this way. "Here lies our path," says Nisus, ". . . I will lay waste all this and lead you on a wide swath" (*'hac iter est . . . et lato te limite ducam'*, 321–3), and he announces the completion of the way (*'via facta per hostis'*, 356). But the way to Aeneas has been cut with shockingly gratuitous slaughter, outdoing by far the Homeric model. Not only has their erotic passion been transformed into the hero's thirst for glory, but, with a shift of elemental balance, the fire of passion rages out of control, as Euryalus too engages in the slaughter (*incensus et ipse / perfurit*, 342–3), until Nisus realizes that their lust for killing has gone too far (*sensit enim nimia caede atque cupidine ferri*, 354 – here is the *dira cupido* he had predicted at the start, 185).

The way to Aeneas has become their metaphorical way to heroic glory, which, unbalanced, has become pure violence. Here is a whole complex of words and associated ideas that is thoroughly Virgilian, but which it is impossible to explore here. Again and again in the *Georgics* Virgil presented the farmer's way (*via*) to discovery and knowledge as force (*vis*) applied to nature, which often becomes excessive force (*violentia*), unbalanced, violating nature. We would expect this complex of verbal associations to appear in the *Aeneid*, but also that, having been so central a part of one of the major themes in the *Georgics*, it would be suggested with restraint. And so it is, as, for example, when Neoptolemus forces an entrance to Priam's palace – *fit via vi* (2.494). For Virgil, in the *Aeneid*, a simple suggestion of this complex of words and ideas is enough. *Via, vis,* and *violentia*: the progress of the two lovers from innocence to heroism – their way to Aeneas – has indeed deceived them, contrary to Nisus' earlier confidence ('*nec nos via fallit euntis*', 243).

The final stage of the mission (367–445) reaches its inevitable climax with the dawn and the first rays of the sun, the *lux inimica* that Nisus had evoked ("Let us stop now, for the day, hostile to us, approaches," 355). But before that, it is still night, and Euryalus has indeed become the Homeric warrior, as he strips the belt, studded with gold (its lineage is given) from Rhamnes and the helmet from Messapus, in a passage of eight lines (359–66): no longer is he the beautiful boy, and once again in the poem armor stripped from a slain enemy is a token of significance. The helmet with its gleam "betrays" Euryalus to a band of Rutulian cavalry "in the shadows of the night" (*sublustri noctis in umbra / prodidit*, 373–4), and the two take to flight into the thickets and "trust in the darkness of night" (*et fidere nocti*, 378). They become separated in the scrubby woods, and "fear deceives them in the direction of their way" (*fallitque timor regione viarum*, 385). Their mission has become a nightmare, as Nisus retraces his way, wandering in the deceptive thickets (*rursus perplexum iter omne revolvens / fallacis silvae simul et vestigia retro / observata legit dumisque silentibus errat*, 391–3). He hears shouts and, too late, sees Euryalus already surrounded by the enemy, "having been overcome by the deception of the place and of night" (*fraude loci et noctis . . . / oppressum*, 397–8).

Euryalus is killed by a sword thrust through the ribs: "blood stains his beautiful limbs and his neck sinks on his shoulder, as when a purple flower, cut down by a plow, withers in death, or as poppies droop, heavy with rain" (434–7). The poppies come from a simile of a similar death in Homer (*Il.* 8.306–8), but the flower cut down by the plow derives from Catullus, as he imagined his love for Lesbia destroyed by her callous unconcern (poem 11.21–4). The flower and the plow, however, are part of a complex of images that go back to Sappho, suggesting ultimately the destruction of the beautiful and innocent by the violence of the heroic world. By combining these two similes here, the Homeric and the Catullan, Virgil has granted Euryalus a hero's death, while at the same time powerfully conveying its brutal senselessness. We will see a related simile soon, of the dead Pallas.

The day comes with full Homeric fanfare (459–60), to reveal just what the night has hidden. The heads of the two victims are paraded on spears before the walls of the Trojan camp, and Euryalus' mother, in her grief at her loss, calls her son "cruel" (*crudelis*, 483) for having betrayed and abandoned her in her old age, wishing to end her "cruel life", just as Evander said he wished to do, should his son Pallas not return from the war (*crudelem abrumpere vitam*, 9.497 = 8.579). Both these anguished speeches are echoes of the words of Catullus' Aegeus, the father of Theseus, at his son's departure on his heroic mission to Crete, the Minotaur, and Ariadne.

Nisus, Euryalus, and his mother are all pathetic victims, deceived, betrayed, and abandoned according to a familiar pattern in Virgil's heroic epic. The fame their deeds have won, though, will be eternal. "Blessed are you both," says Virgil in one of his rare apostrophes. "If my song (*mea carmina*) has any power, no day will ever forget you, so long as the house of Aeneas inhabits the firm rock of the Capitol and the Roman senator holds power" (446–9). The death of these two lovers and the grief of a mother seem to have been pre-empted by the cause of imperial Rome, but in the context of all that we have just listened to in Virgil's song, we are permitted to hear in this proud prediction a tone of ambivalent irony.

Pallas and Lausus

Pallas and Lausus presented Virgil with a problem, though we might also see it as an opportunity for the sort of ambiguity he was so fond of. Italy itself, as we will soon discuss, had to unite two apparent contradictions: it had to be a worthy martial opponent of the Trojans, a people experienced in 10 years of daily battle, but at the same time, in Virgil's conception, it also had to be a land of inherent peace and innocence, to which the Trojans brought strife. Similarly, Pallas and Lausus had to be fighters with enough skill and strength to be credible opponents to Turnus and Aeneas, but at the same time, in Virgil's mind, were to be further victims of the world of iron. For Virgil this was not an impossible contradiction. Like Nisus and Euryalus, Pallas (especially) and Lausus are drawn into the heroic world through a sort of initiation, but, once engaged in the reality of combat, they are overmatched by superior strength and in death become part of the pattern of innocence destroyed.

We see Pallas first at the beginning of Book VIII, at the site of future Rome, where Aeneas has come seeking help from King Evander. The Tiber has stayed its current, allowing the ships an easy passage upstream. Two details, typically Virgilian, are worth noting. First, we are reminded again that Aeneas is bringing war to a peaceful land: the waves and "the unaccustomed woods" wonder (*mirantur . . . / miratur* – verbs that connote a reaction to anything unnatural, from awe to horror) at "the flashing arms of the men and at the painted hulls" (*fulgentia longe / scuta virum fluvio pictasque innare carinas*, 8.90–3). Some readers have been reminded of the beginning of Catullus' epyllion (poem 64), where the Nereids wonder at the first warship to sail the seas, carrying the Argonauts and Jason, marking the beginning of the age of heroes and all that will follow; and in any case, we hear again Virgil's *Leitmotif* of heroism, *scuta virum*. Second, the calm naturalism of the riparian scene (95–6) gives way, on the arrival of the Trojans, to the fiery heat of the midday sun (*sol medium caeli conscenderat igneus orbem*, 97).

The Arcadians are celebrating the festival of Hercules when the warships appear, a terrifying sight (*terrentur visu subito*, 109). It is Pallas who, dramatically, seizes a spear and runs to meet them – "Who are you? From whence? Do you bring war or peace?" (110–14). Aeneas answers, and Pallas is "struck with awe at so great a name" (121). Pallas seems poised, as we first see him, between the primitivistic peace of Saturnian Italy and the heroic warfare that Aeneas represents.

Aeneas is received by Evander according to a Homeric pattern (152–74) and aid is promised (*'auxilio laetos dimittam opibusque iuvabo'*, 171 – almost the identical formula with which Dido had promised her help, 1.571). The ritual feast of Hercules concluded, Evander takes Aeneas through the site of Rome, once a scene of Saturn's Golden Age and primitivistic peace (as we will see later), with war and greed only lately arrived (314–36): Evander is showing Aeneas the character of his land.

The next morning they meet again, and after relating the inhuman brutality of the Etruscan tyrant Mezentius, Evander entrusts his son to Aeneas, to learn from him "war and the grave work of Mars, to observe your deeds, and to admire you from his early years" (514–17). The significance of the moment is underlined by the reaction of Aeneas and Achates to Evander's proposal – intent silence, as Aeneas reflects upon the harsh reality of war (*defixique ora tenebant . . . multaque dura suo tristi cum corde putabant*, 520, 522). And then a sign from Venus – lighting and thunder in a clear sky, and arms flashing in the heavens, trumpets sounding. Aeneas recognizes and accepts the omen as promising slaughter of the Latins and punishment for Turnus: "How many shields of men and helmets and mighty bodies will you roll beneath your waves, father Tiber" (*'quam multa sub undas / scuta virum galeasque et fortia corpora volves, / Thybri pater'*, 538–40 – and again the *Leitmotif* of heroic battle, *scuta virum*, is sounded). The omens at a similar impasse at Troy (the fire springing from Iulus' head and the confirming shooting star) initiated the first steps of the Roman mission (2.679–704). These omens mark a further and far more terrible stage. We think, too, of the Simois in the *Iliad*, choked with the bodies of those slaughtered by Achilles in his rampage after Patroclus had been killed, and we anticipate Aeneas' fury and mad slaughter brought on by Pallas' death.

Pallas has been sent to learn war from Aeneas, to be initiated into deeds of arms, and the omens sent by Venus show exactly what this war will become. There is a wonderful cameo (10.159–62), as Aeneas and the Etruscan fleet sail down the coast of Italy on their way to the besieged Trojan camp. It is night. "Great Aeneas" sits in his ship, pondering on the vicissitudes of war (*eventus belli varios*), with Pallas close on his left, "asking now about the stars, the road of dark night, and [Aeneas'] sufferings on land and sea" (*iam quaerit sidera, opacae / noctis iter, iam quae passus terraque marique*). "The road of dark night" is somewhat unclear, usually taken in apposition with "the stars," and it may be that Pallas is simply getting his first lesson in navigational astronomy; but after Nisus and Euryalus and their attempt to find a way to Aeneas through the night, it is hard not to feel in this *iter* a premonition of what must follow.

Pallas learned well. The battle in Book X begun, he urges on his hard-pressed Arcadians with appeals to past brave deeds, Evander's reputation and victories, and his own promise as a warrior, avid for glory (10.369–71). His *aristeia* (362–425) is everything that his father might wish to see. Lausus meets him, but Jupiter does not allow them to fight, since each is fated to fall at the hands of a greater enemy (426–38). Turnus comes on, claiming Pallas for himself, and wishing that Evander were there to witness the combat (442–3). It is no contest, and Pallas is killed like a Homeric hero (in four lines of striking Homeric formulae, 486–9). Pallas dies a hero's death, and this may be what Turnus acknowledges when he says, over the corpse, "Such as [Evander] deserved, this is the Pallas I send back to him" (492). Turnus strips the body of its baldric but allows the honor of burial – perfectly acceptable, even generous, heroic behavior.

But moralizing and fault-finding are rampant here too. The reactions of many readers are similar to those evoked when Aeneas leaves Dido. Turnus' words and actions have been seen as boastful and arrogant, and his stripping of the baldric has been taken as the great fault (his *culpa*, even) that was finally, and justly, punished by Aeneas. All this is not only questionable, but can distract us from what Virgil does show us.

Pallas receives an apostrophe at his death, just as had Nisus and Euryalus in the previous book. "O you returning to your father, a grief and a great glory, / this day first gave you to battle and took you from it, / although you leave behind huge heaps of Rutulian dead" (507–9). Each line presents a distinct idea. To Evander, his son's initiation to heroism is a source both of glory and anguish; Pallas died young, in his first experience of war; and war is savagery. These "huge heaps of Rutulian dead" are just what Aeneas' savagery will produce in his *aristeia* that follows. There is no moralizing here.

In death, Pallas becomes not just the slain warrior, but as well the beautiful boy, like Euryalus. On the day after the great battle of Book X, the dead are taken up. Aeneas' first concern is that Pallas be sent home, "whom, not lacking in heroic courage, a black day has taken from us and sunk in bitter death" ('*quem non virtutis egentem / abstulit atra dies et funere mersit acerbo*', 11.27–8): line 28 occurred earlier, applied to the infants whose crying Aeneas hears in the Underworld (6.429). Aeneas addresses the pale corpse of Pallas (*nivei Pallantis*, 11.39, where the epithet may be an etymological gloss on the proper name) as "boy to be pitied" (*miserande puer*, 42 – and so too he had just addressed Lausus, 10.825), but Virgil's real focus is on the bier and the body upon it. The bier itself is a purposefully rustic construction, shaded with branches, "a rustic litter" (*agresti stramine*, 67), and, moreover, woven of the two materials that are emblematic, not only throughout Virgil but generally, of a primitive time in man's history, the arbute and the oak, the source of sustenance before the arts of Ceres produced grain crops (*molle feretrum / arbuteis texunt virgis et vimine querno*, 64–5). Virgil returns us here to the pre-Trojan primitivism and peace with which the Pallas episode began (8.91–3).

The youth (*iuvenem*) lies on the bier "like a flower plucked by a maiden's thumb, either of a delicate violet or a withering hyacinth, and while it still retains its aura and form, the earth its mother no longer nourishes it and provides strength" (68–71). The beauty and the power of this simile depend on its recall of contexts in the wedding poems of Catullus (61.56–9, 87–9, 186–8; 62.21–2, 39–47), which go back as well to Sappho. The bride is always the delicate growth, uprooted from its protecting and sustaining garden, torn away and despoiled by the bridegroom. To the same sphere belongs the simile of Euryalus in death, "the purple flower cut down by the plow, wilting in death" (9.435–6, and see above). Virgil then reminds us of another victim: Aeneas brings forth two cloaks as "a final honor for the youth," which "Dido had made and had woven in a fine gold thread," one of them the very cloak which Aeneas had worn at Carthage in happy days. So it would seem, or so we are made to feel, since *Dido / fecerat et tenui telas discreverat auro* (11.74–5) is repeated from 4.263–4.

At this point we need not say much about Evander, whose two speeches (the first as he sends Pallas off with Aeneas, 8.560–83, and the second as he receives his son's body, 11.152–81) echo the anguish of Euryalus' mother (9.481–97) and sound again the Catullan themes of loss and betrayal in the new age of heroes.

Lausus is a less successful character, generally, among these young victims, perhaps simply because he is less fully developed. He is the child of a parent, and just as Euryalus' mother seems to be there because she is needed to complete the full picture of her son, so Lausus seems to be essential for Mezentius' conversion, another variation of the theme of *pietas*. In some aspects, too, he seems merely complementary to Pallas. At this point we need not try to make the connections all over again: I will simply point to some of the essential themes.

The catalogue of Italians in Book VII begins with Mezentius, *contemptor divum* ("despiser of the gods"), the tyrant from Etruscan Caere, whom Evander will portray as the incarnation of despotic evil, but he receives only two lines (7.647–8) here. Lausus is given 6 lines (649–54): he is both handsome (*pulchrior*) – indeed, more beautiful than all others with the exception of Turnus – and a warrior-hunter (*equum domitor debellatorque ferarum*).

As the battle rages in Book X, Pallas and Lausus are poised to meet, "close in age, outstanding in beauty, but to whom Fortune had denied return home" (434–6). Lausus does not appear again until his father has been seriously wounded by Aeneas. "When he saw this, Lausus groaned from love of his dear father and tears rolled down his cheeks" (789–90) – and Virgil suddenly interrupts the narrative for an apostrophe of three lines (791–3), addressing Lausus (*iuvenis memorande*) and promising him poetic fame, just as he does to Nisus, Euryalus, and Pallas. Lausus comes between Mezentius and Aeneas and allows his father to retreat. Under a rain of javelins, Aeneas taunts and threatens Lausus. "Your piety deceives you, incautious" (*'fallit te incautum pietas tua'*, 812), but the fury of war has taken possession of them both. Aeneas drives his sword through Lausus' shield and "the tunic which his mother had woven with soft gold" (*et tunicam molli mater quam neverat auro*, 818), and with this we are again in the presence of Euryalus' mother and of Dido. The savage anger of the hero (*saevae iamque altius irae / Dardanio surgunt ductori*, 813–4) has claimed another victim.

The fury of Aeneas' *aristeia* that had begun with Pallas' death now suddenly ends, with the killing of this complementary figure. Aeneas, designated now by his patronymic, looks at the face of the dying Lausus, "strangely pale": *at vero ut vultum vidit morientis et ora, / ora modis*

Anchisiades pallentia miris (821–2). *Pallentia* may be more than stock epithet here: it may be an etymological gloss on the name Pallas, anticipating *nivei Pallantis*, 11.39, noted above. Aeneas is struck by the image of filial piety; he groans and reaches out his right hand. He addresses the boy (*miserande puer*, 825) and grants him his arms and burial, but there is no human consolation he can offer, only an appeal to heroism, that "you fall at the hands of great Aeneas" (830).

Lausus' body is brought back to Mezentius, who replays (846–56) the themes of the speeches of Euryalus' mother and Evander – that heroism has caused, in an inversion of the natural order, parents to see the death of a child, leaving them bereft in their old age. But he also feels remorse for his past crimes, and, unlike the other two parents, he can die (855–6). He returns to face death at the hands of Aeneas, which some have seen as a redemption. His own final words to Aeneas (*'hostis amare'*, as he addresses him, "bitter enemy," 900) ask only for protection from his enemies and burial with his son, and as he accepts Aeneas' thrust, he appears indeed to have learned something (*haud inscius*, 907) that we cannot quite feel any certainty about. We see only another death, futile and empty.

Some Aspects of Turnus

There seems to be no more purpose to Turnus' death than there is to Mezentius', and it is certainly no redemption.

Turnus is the greatest fighter of the Italians, ever, as he himself freely boasts (*'Turnus ego, haud ulli veterum virtute secundus'*, 11.441). The Sibyl had nominated him "another Achilles" (6.89–90), but he is now Virgil's Hector, the greatest fighter of Troy, when, for instance, he kills Pallas (a surrogate Patroclus) or when he defends Latinus' city and falls outside its walls at the hands of a surrogate Achilles. This is obvious, and therefore, like much that is obvious, we don't think much more about it, and we may not think much more when Virgil gives us Aeneas in the obvious role of the great enemy of Troy, Achilles, as he does, for instance, in Aeneas' *aristeia* in Book X. But surely, if we tend to reduce the major figures of Virgil's epic to the good and the bad, we ought to pay attention when Turnus becomes the Trojan Hector or Aeneas the Greek Achilles. These are not minor details, and Virgil was not a mindless manipulator of his Homeric precedents.

Turnus is Aeneas' great opponent and thus his enemy and the enemy of Rome, opposing fate at every turn and blocking the march of progress, and therefore he must be bad, his death must certainly be deserved, and his defeat has to be a triumph for Rome. That is the black-and-white picture,

and it is often the basis of a common perception of Turnus, and one easy
to support in the poem. Turnus is all violence (*violentia*), rash boldness
(*audacia*), and confidence in his own might (*fiducia*) – in other words, a
fighter through and through, heedless of what grief his own self-interest is
causing his people. There is some truth to what Drances says (11.336–75).
Book XII opens with a vivid picture of Turnus, the object of his people's
stares, burning with implacable spirit like a Carthaginian lion, wounded
but all the more fierce; his characteristic violence grows (*accenso gliscit
violentia Turno*, 12.9), and he exists in an irrational whirl of emotion (*tur-
bidus*, 10). And even if Drances has his bias, we ought to trust Latinus, who
credits Turnus' courage but seems to caution against its wild impetuosity
('*o praestans animi iuvenis, quantum ipse feroci / virtute exsuperas*', 19–20).
A convincing case against Turnus can be made; after all, Virgil intended
that it be easily made.

In our own brief discussion of the Roman concept of character in the
previous chapter, we suggested that it was possible for a Roman to see an
individual's *ingenium* (what is "inborn") as fixed and unalterable and that
apparent change was a matter not of a change of character but of behavior, due often to an altered environment. Seen another way, an individual's
nature, like his body and like everything else in the physical world, is made
up of a few elementary oppositions; when the mixture is proper and the
oppositions are in balance, all goes well, but when, again due to environment, imbalance occurs, then all is less than well. But it is still the same
individual we are observing, just as there is only one *virtus*, one ideal of
heroic courage, whether it leads to noble and admirable deeds or, when
the fire of its basic nature comes to dominate, to savage slaughter. We have
considered some scenes where the assumption of such a view might be
useful or helpful in understanding Aeneas, and we will now see if it helps
in deepening our appreciation of Turnus.

Turnus is the dominant figure of the second half of the *Aeneid*, and most
of what we need to know about him is given at intervals in Book VII. We
learn first that he was the foremost suitor for the hand of Lavinia, "most
handsome before all others, distinguished in lineage" (*ante alios pulcher-
rimus omnis / Turnus, avis atavisque potens*, 7.55–6): beauty and nobility
– just what is required of a royal son-in-law.

Allecto's visit and torch have had the desired effect: "Mad, [Turnus] calls
for arms; . . . love of the sword rages, and the accursed madness of war, and
anger beyond all" (*arma amens fremit . . . ; / saevit amor ferri et scelerata
insania belli, / ira super*, 460–2). This is the beginning of his *violentia*, his
ferox virtus, but for Virgil it is only the beginning. The passage ends with
the response of the Rutulians whom he calls to arms: "his outstanding
beauty and youth move one, his royal ancestry another, and another his

prowess in feats of arms" (*hunc decus egregium formae movet atque iuventae, / hunc atavi reges, hunc claris dextera factis*, 473–4): youthful beauty, nobility, and deeds.

These two lines have not received the attention they deserve, for they have a specific reference and sphere: they point directly to the traditional qualities of a Roman aristocrat. The ideal of the Roman aristocracy was in many ways very similar to the world of the Mycenean heroes. Birth and family were essential for membership in the club, and with this comes the unquestioned assumption of excellence, both of inborn character (*ingenium* again) and of physical beauty; and, from the *virtus* that is the inherited possession of the aristocrat, the words and deeds expected of him inevitably follow. Even if an individual dies young, it can be assumed and noted in his epitaph that he would have gone on to hold the highest offices and to do great things. Hence, whenever there is an opportunity for "the praises of famous men" (*laudes clarorum virorum*), the form is generally the same.

The memory of the great man is most succinctly preserved in his epitaph, cut in stone. The funeral oration can be seen as an expansion of the epitaph, and the literary-historical biography (such as Suetonius' *Lives*) is a further expansion. The basic elements, though, remain the same. First, most obviously, there is the name of the commemorated, in the epitaph always given with his father's name; in the expanded forms, the family and its character can receive further attention. Then there is usually a formulaic reminder of the deceased's inborn *virtus* (in the epitaph, such epithets as *fortis, fidelis, sapiens* are conventional). Finally, there is the enumeration of offices held and deeds accomplished (*facta*). Our oldest examples of aristocratic epitaphs are those of the Scipios, all of which can be seen today in the Chiaramonte Museum in the Vatican (near Bramante's staircase) and are well worth searching out. (They can be read most conveniently in the Loeb Classical Library volume of *Remains of Old Latin* vol. IV ['Archaic Inscriptions'], pp. 2–8.) The first of these is the well-known epitaph of Scipio Barbatus, consul in 298 BC, written in archaizing Latin in Saturnian verses:

Cornelius Lucius Scipio Barbatus
Gnaivod patre prognatus, fortis vir sapiensque,
quoius forma virtutei parisuma fuit,
consol censor aidilis quei fuit apud vos
Taurasia Cisauna Samnio cepit,
subigit omne Loucanam opsidesque abdoucit.

Lucius Cornelius Scipio Barbatus,
son of Gnaeus, a brave man and wise,

whose appearance was very like his aristocratic quality (*virtus*),
who was consul, censor, aedile while with you:
he captured Taurasia and Cisauna in Samnium (?),
he subdued all of Lucania and took hostages.

The form is clear – name and family, aristocratic qualities, then offices and deeds. "A brave and wise man" (*fortis vir sapiensque*) sums up the essential quality of both Homeric hero and Roman aristocrat – someone excellent in deed and word, action and speech. But what will be of special interest to us is the assumption that such a man will be physically handsome (his *forma*) as well as generally excellent (his *virtus*). Note too that the list of his military achievements is given as a series of simple statements (accusatives and verbs usually in the perfect tense).

For a second example we can do no better than Trimalchio's own epitaph (Petronius, *Satyricon*, 71.12), a wonderful parody of the form that is still perfectly preserved some three and a half centuries after the time of Scipio Barbatus:

C. Pompeius Trimalchio Maecenatianus hic requiescit.
huic seviratus absenti decretus est; cum posset in omnibus
decuriis Romae esset, tamen noluit. pius, fortis, fidelis.
ex parvo crevit; sestertium reliquit trecenties,
nec umquam philosophum audivit. Vale et tu.

Gaius Pompeius Trimalchio Maecenatianus lies here.
He was elected in absence to the priesthood of Augustus; he could have held office at Rome, but declined. Pious, brave, faithful.
He started from nothing, and left three hundred million sesterces, and he never listened to a philosopher. Farewell to you, too.

Here too is the full name – in this case that of a freed slave, posing as the nobility. Then he recites his offices (which he did not choose to hold). Then there is the formula for the character of the aristocrat (*pius, fortis, fidelis*). And finally the deeds – his amassing of a huge fortune, and the proud boast of happy, uneducated ignorance. Later, at the very end of the banquet that has become a rehearsal for his own funeral, he pronounces his own *elogium* (75.8).

Many more relevant examples could be given and much more could be said, but it should be clear that the Rutulians' response to Turnus' call to arms (473–4) is based on a form that every Roman would instinctively perceive and react to: his lineage (*atavi reges*), his aristocratic qualities (*decus egregium formae . . . atque iuventae* – and more about this peculiar variation later), and his deeds (*claris dextera factis*). From this certain observations follow.

First, Turnus is thoroughly Roman, in the pattern of the great aristocratic Roman families who traced their lines back to the beginning of the Republic and even beyond. We should hesitate, then, to put him too casually among the enemies of Rome. It has been noticed that Dido, nearing her end, also writes her own epitaph and in so doing, for a moment at least, becomes herself thoroughly Roman. She has mounted the pyre and, lying on the couch, addresses the tokens of her life with Aeneas: "I have lived my life and followed the course Fortune granted me: . . . I founded my city, I saw my walls, I avenged my husband, punishing my brother" (*vixi et quem dederat cursum fortuna peregi: . . . urbem praeclaram statui, mea moenia vidi, / ulta virum poenas inimico a fratre recepi*, 4.653, 655–6). In Latin the form is unmistakable – the simplicity of the accusative direct objects and the perfect tenses of the simple verbs is exactly that of the epitaph of Scipio Barbatus or (to add another example) that of the splendid old Appius Claudius Caecus, consul in 307 and 296 BC: *complura oppida de Samnitibus cepit. Sabinorum et Tuscorum exercitum fudit. pacem fieri cum Pyrrho rege prohibuit. in censura viam Appiam stravit et aquam in urbem adduxit. aedem Bellonae fecit* (CIL I p. 287).

Just who are these royal ancestors of Turnus that we have twice heard about (7.56 and 474)? They are not just the rulers of Ardea, but of Argos too, as Amata reminds Latinus: "And to Turnus, if the origin of his line is traced, there is Inachus and Acrisius and central Mycenae" (371–2). Family is character, and since character was unchanging, lineage was extremely important for a Roman, as we have suggested. The origin (the source, quite literally) of Argos is Inachus, the river god, well known to us because of his daughter Io, who, becoming the object of Zeus' passion and Hera's jealousy, was turned into a cow and driven by Hera's gadfly in a maddened flight to Egypt. There, four generations later, the brothers Danaus (he of the 50 daughters) and Aegyptus (of the 50 sons) appear on the scene. Danaus returns to rule in his ancestral Argos, where, several generations later, Acrisius, inheriting the rule along with his brother Proetus, has a daughter named Danae. And she again, in what seems to have been a family tradition, became the object of Zeus' lust, who visited her in the famous shower of gold. This form of disguise was necessary because Acrisius had shut her up in a tower of bronze, heeding a prophecy that her son would kill his grandfather, and so when Danae conceived and Perseus was born (though he might have been fathered by Proetus, some said), Acrisius shut the two of them up this time in a chest and sent it off on the sea. One variant in the tradition has it that Danae actually came ashore in Latium and there, with a new royal husband, founded Ardea (so Servius notes on 7.372). The history of Argos and its ruling family, even in this outline, had everything one could want: fraternal strife, divine passion, metamorphoses, forced marriage and mass murder, the lust for rule and power and its consequences.

Danae is brought to our attention again in Book VII when Allecto comes on her dusky wings to Ardea, "a city which Danae, borne on the headlong south wind, is said (*dicitur*, a signpost marking an aetiology) to have founded with settlers descended from Acrisius" (409–11). We should add, too, what might seem a bit of gratuitous learning (in Virgil there is no such thing), that when Juno arrives in Italy to stir up all the trouble in Book VII, she "was returning from Inachian Argos" (*Ecce autem Inachiis sese referebat ab Argis / saeva Iovis coniunx*, 286–7). We should also note how purposeful Virgil is in these references, how much he leaves out (the several generations in Egypt after Io – Epaphus, Libye, Belus – or any mention of Perseus), and how he focuses repeatedly on certain figures (especially Inachus, Acrisius, and Danae).

Virgil's purpose begins to emerge at the end of Book VII, with Turnus as the next-to-last entry in the catalogue of Italians. Eight lines are devoted to his helmet and shield and the two emblems appearing on each. On his triple-plumed helmet the monster Chimaera is represented belching fire and flame, which become more intense as battles become the bloodier (*cui [Turno] triplici crinita iuba galea alta Chimaeram / sustinet Aetnaeos efflantem faucibus ignis; / tam magis illa fremens et tristibus effera flammis / quam magis effuso crudescunt sanguine pugnae*, 785–8). But in opposition to the fire on his helmet, water dominates on his shield. There is Io, with raised horns, in gold, already becoming a cow, "a vast theme" (*argumentum ingens*), and Argus on guard, and her river-god father, Inachus, pouring his river water from an urn (789–92). There is divinity in ever-flowing water in the Mediterranean world, for obvious reasons: Inachus is the source of life, properly then the original founder of Argos, opposing the monstrous Chimaera's destroying fire, just as Troy's Simois opposed Achilles and his fire. Turnus bears two emblems, one of war, but the other of civilization and peace, and we should not forget this.

That Turnus goes into battle with the metamorphosing Io on his shield, though, is something that might be difficult for modern readers to accept, and certainly to understand, and yet Virgil would not have set her there without good reason, nor would he have marked her appearance as "a vast subject, theme" (*argumentum ingens*). The key, surely, lies with Calvus' epyllion *Io*, and unfortunately this influential poem did not survive the chances of transmission. Calvus was a friend of Catullus and was recognized as an equally important poet, whose masterwork was significant enough for Virgil to quote directly several times in the *Eclogues* (e.g., 2.69; 6.47, 52, with the comment of Servius on 6.47): Io is the paradigm of the madness (*dementia*) of erotic passion, and her metamorphosis would seem to be an emblem of bestial lust. Ovid tells the story of Io with characteristic humor (*Met.* 1.582–746), but it is hard to see in his telling what might have been so compelling in Calvus' poem, for Virgil and others. As Virgil suggests, Calvus' Io was the exemplar of erotic *furor* and ensuing madness: the gadfly is a source of madness in *Georgics* III (where it has picked up an accretion of Hellenistic reference) and is associated with elemental fire, driving the herds mad in the heat of midday. Io indeed seems to have been an *argumentum ingens*; though the details must remain cloudy, the associations we can gather from these and other clues are clear, and we must take her seriously as a "vast theme." We can add one final point of significance. In the *Georgics* Virgil begins to apply the adjective *ingens* to things that are often rather small, hardly huge or vast, and it is clear in most cases that he is playing on the etymological significance of the word (as if from *ingenium*) to connote "the inborn character" of the thing modified. Io's story, so marked, has something to tell us about the character of the hero whose shield bears her representation.

There is another related story that we need to mention here. Turnus stands over the corpse of Pallas, stripping it of the "huge weight of the baldric" (*immania pondera baltei*, 10.496) and "its embossed crime" (*impressumque nefas*, 497) – "the band of youths foully slaughtered on their wedding night and the bloody marriage chambers." The scene on the belt, in which Turnus now rejoices, is that of the murder of the 50 sons of Aegyptus by their cousins, the daughters of Danaus, a crime of passion for which the Danaids (or 49 of them, at least) are still punished in the Underworld. *Impressumque nefas* has the ring of *argumentum ingens* and is another story in the long history of Turnus' Argos which he will carry into battle from this point on, another reminder of how close are the madness of war and the madness of erotic passion. Finally, it does not take a particularly close or subtle reading of the last lines of the *Aeneid* to see that this "embossed crime" is what is referred to when Virgil tells us that the defeated Turnus "was bearing on his shoulders a fatal mark" (*inimicum insigne*, 12.944) – difficult to translate, but certainly not designating just the belt itself. Aeneas' attention, as he stands hesitating over Turnus, is not directed only at Pallas' baldric ("the spoils," *exuvias*) but at what is shown upon it, the *saevi monumenta doloris*, another phrase hard to translate, "the everlasting memorials of the savagery of passion gone wrong" (945). We see this precedent just as does Aeneas, and accordingly the hero acts, "set aflame by madness, terrible in his anger."

There is one other aspect of Turnus still to be considered, and that is his appearance, the *decus egregium formae . . . atque iuventae* that some of his followers are moved by (7.473), his youthful beauty. In Book XII, though, this aristocratic attribute that he shares with Scipio Barbatus becomes something quite different.

The beginning of the last book belongs entirely to Turnus, to his growing *violentia* (12.9, 45) and *ferox virtus* (19–20). But in the first exchange between Latinus and Turnus (10–53), there is a strange undertone of erotic language – nothing explicit, but rather an unsettling succession of words and phrases that could easily occur together in an amatory context. And Latinus ends his plea with an appeal to Turnus' pity for his aged father (*'miserere parentis / longaevi, quem nunc maestum patria Ardea longe / dividit'*, 43–5), another aged father who is about to lose a son.

The next scene is stranger still, suffused with an eroticism that defies logical explanation and hence exerts an unnerving power over the reader. There is something going on here between Amata, Lavinia, and Turnus that we do not understand and that we are not meant to understand: we sense, rather, undercurrents of emotion that run counter to the outward, observable words and actions of the heroes in the world of clear values that we think we know. Only Virgil knew how to do this.

At regina . . . conterrita . . . moritura (54–5): "But the queen . . ." is Dido's theme, and Amata here, trying to keep Turnus with her, fearful in her knowledge of what must be and of her own death, forces us to remember the Carthaginian queen; her first words of entreaty to Turnus reinforce this impression (compare 12.56–7 with 4.314–19 – exact recall would destroy the effect). We must remember the beginning, the very first we heard of Amata's "strange-and-wonderful love" for her future son-in-law (*Turnus . . . quem regia coniunx / adiungi generum miro properabat amore*, 7.56–7). But Virgil doesn't allow us to try to sort this out, in any logical way (none of this is logical), because Amata continues with another appeal, "You are now my only hope for the future, you are the source of rest and peace for my weary old age" (*spes tu nunc una, senectae / tu requies miserae*, 57–8), and with these words we remember Euryalus' mother, Evander, Mezentius, and Catullus' Aegeus, parents who lived to see the death of a child.

Amata ends her short speech with the promise to die if Turnus is killed. Lavinia's reaction is immediate and again below the level of logical explanation: she receives her mother's words with tears and a blush that runs over her fevered cheeks with fire, like ivory stained with blood-red purple or like the red of roses mixed with lilies (64–9). What is it that has so stirred her, an otherwise totally passive, voiceless, and almost nonexistent character, and why this simile of ivory stained with purple, which comes from the blood flowing over Menelaus' wounded thigh (*Il.* 4.141–7)? Does she blush that her mother has revealed her own feelings – erotic as well as maternal – for Turnus so clearly? Or is it her own passion that we see, again the fire and the wound of love? Do we sense that the fire of love and the fire of war are coinciding yet again in the poem, and that Lavinia's tears are for the death that is now inevitable? Whatever it may be, her love strikes Turnus with a confusion of emotion as he sees Lavinia's blush, and he burns with a passion – but a passion for war (*illum turbat amor figitque in virgine vultus; / ardet in arma magis*, 70–1). So much is happening in this extraordinary scene, so many conflicting undercurrents of emotion are felt in each of these participants that converge with other scenes, other figures, throughout the poem. Only Virgil could do this.

To continue. The terms for the single combat between Aeneas and Turnus have been arranged. The stage is set, grandly, with both Trojans and Italians as spectators, with the entrance of Latinus and Turnus in their chariots, and Aeneas and Ascanius ("the second hope for great Rome"), with priests and sacrificial animals (161–74). A solemn prayer is offered by Aeneas, then by Latinus, sanctifying the terms of settlement, and the ritual sacrifice is performed (175–215). The occasion of a single combat on which everything hangs is one that Roman historians make the most of, and Virgil's preparations remind one of similar scenes in Livy, when the future of Rome hangs in the balance and two armies watch in suspense. We could easily imagine all this on the operatic stage. Two great warriors are to meet to settle the fate of two warring peoples collected from all of Italy.

Only if we appreciate the dramatic grandeur and the rhetorical richness of this setting will we be prepared to react to what happens next, in just six lines (216–21). There are no longer two great champions, two giant figures ready to do combat like two great bulls (in the similes of 12.103–6 and 715–22). Suddenly, one is but a youth, with almost maidenly modesty, and no match at all for the warrior. "But indeed to the Rutulians this combat began to seem unfair, and their hearts were variously moved, then all the more as they observed more closely how unequal in might were the combatants, a feeling heightened by Turnus as he approached the altar with silent step, praying as a suppliant with lowered gaze, with the down still on his cheeks, his youthful body pale." The details are remarkable: his gait (*incessu tacito*) and lowered eyes (*demisso lumine*) are the common attributes of the modesty of a young girl, and his cheeks (*pubentes genae*) and the whiteness of his boyish body (*iuvenali in corpore pallor*) are appropriate not to a hardened fighter, but to a beautiful boy.

Neither Turnus nor Aeneas is a simple character. Virgil composed them of various and varying elements, never stable, never remaining in a predictable balance, but with the constituent elements always recognizable.

The destroying fire of the Chimaera on Turnus' helmet is balanced by the water poured out by the life-giving river Inachus, and his characteristic *violentia* in war is of the same composition, the same mixture, as the prototypical exemplars of sexual madness (*dementia, furor*) of Io or the Danaids, his ancestors. His aristocratic appearance (*decus egregium formae . . . atque iuventae*) at one time attracts the Rutulians to follow him to war, at another time to pity him just as Euryalus, Pallas, and Lausus were to be pitied at their deaths, for the waste of their youth and beauty. There is no final message to be abstracted here, no conclusions to be drawn about the rightness or wrongness of Turnus' actions or of what his heroic world made of him.

Camilla

When Turnus died, "his life departed with a groan, complaining, to the shades below" (*vitaque cum gemitu fugit indignata sub umbras*, the final line of the epic), and precisely so does Camilla die (12.952 = 11.831), and so do the souls of Patroclus and Hector depart in the *Iliad* ("his soul flew forth from his limbs and went to Hades' house, bemoaning its fate, leaving manhood and youth," *Il.* 16.856–7 = 22.362–3).

Camilla is another victim of the progress to Rome. She seems to be Virgil's own invention. Her name is obscure but has religious overtones: by Virgil's time *camillus* (*camilla*) was used only of a young boy or girl who had a role in certain rituals. Virgil's Camilla is the type of Amazonian warrior-maiden, like Penthesilea, who fought at Troy (1.490–3), but she is also the type of virgin devotee of Diana, such as Venus had pretended to be (1.314–20). She is a figure of mythic unreality, with the ability to speed over fields of grain leaving the heads untouched, or over the sea with dry foot, faster than the very winds (7.807–11). As the maiden huntress she avoids entirely the world of men and marriage, and as the Amazonian warrior "she dares, a virgin, mix in battle with men" (*audetque viris concurrere virgo*, 1.493, of Penthesilea).

It is she, not Turnus, who has the honor of closing the catalogue of Italians in Book VII (803–17). There she is introduced as a warrior (*bellatrix*, as was Penthesilea), not accustomed to spinning and the work of Minerva, but "as a girl to endure harsh battle and to outstrip the winds in speed of foot." She is the wonder of the rural population as she passes – with a cloak of royal purple and a golden pin binding her hair, a discordant note: these are not the possessions of one who belongs to the natural world. But she also has the usual quiver and (closing the catalogue) "a shepherd's staff of myrtle tipped with a spear head" (7.817).

Diana relates the story of Camilla to Opis (11.535–94). Camilla was an infant when her father Metabus, king of Privernum, was driven out of his city by the hostility of his citizens (much like Mezentius) at his arrogant misuse of power. Closely pursued, the babe in his arms, he is halted by a river in spate. What to do? He fashions a cradle of cork, ties it with bark to his mighty spear, and hurls her safely across the flood. From an urban life and royal power misused, he now becomes a man of nature: "No cities received him with roofs and walls, nor would he, given his wildness (*feritate*), surrender, but he lived the life of shepherds in the lonely mountains" (567–9). There his daughter grows up, fed on mare's milk, armed from her first steps with javelins and arrows, and instead of golden ornaments for her hair and woman's dress, she wears a tiger's skin, having regard only for the weapons and virginity of Diana. All the elements are in place.

Camilla is the closest Virgil got to allegory. There was "the life of shepherds in the lonely mountains" in her childhood, and then her devotion (literally, for her father offered her as a servant to Diana on the bank of the raging river, 557–60) to virginity, Diana, and the hunt. But the weapons of the huntress become the weapons of war, and "in vain is she girt with our weapons," says Diana, marking the transition (535–6). By the time Camilla becomes the warrior-maiden, she has acquired the purple cloak in place of the tiger skin of her childhood and a golden ornament for her hair, which she had specifically scorned as a girl (576–7), and she has armed herself with a golden bow (652). She represents the passage from the natural world to war and wealth.

Her *aristeia* (664–724) consists of the usual list of the slaughtered, with two longer accounts of her victims, both significant. The first (677–89) is a hunter, a wild man dressed in the skin of a bullock and a wolf's-head helmet, whom she kills and taunts for thinking that war was the same as hunting (*'silvis te, Tyrrhene, feras agitare putasti?'*, 686). The second, a nameless warrior from the Apennines in Liguria, seeing that he has no escape as she sets upon him, deceives her into fighting on foot and then flees on his horse when she has dismounted – to no avail, of course (699–724). The vivid scene is focused on deceit and deception (*fallere*, 701; *dolos et astu*, 704; *fraudem*, 708; *dolo*, 712; *lubricus*, 716; *fraus . . . fallaci*, 717). Like Nisus and Euryalus, and equally out of place, Camilla enters a heroic world marked by deception, and her own will follow.

Camilla's end needs no explication. She is tracked by a certain Arruns (*tacitus vestigia lustrat*, 763), the huntress becoming the hunted, as he pursues her with cunning and guile (*multa arte*, 760; *furtim*, 765). She has lost all caution, attracted by the rich garments of a Trojan priest, Chloreus, all resplendent in purple and gold (Virgil devotes 10 lines to the description of his elaborate dress, 768–77), "whether she intended to fix the Trojan arms as a temple offering or to dress herself in captured gold, though a huntress" (*sive ut templi praefigeret arma / Troia, captivo sive ut se ferret in auro / venatrix*, 778–80). She is blinded, incautious, "burning with a womanly love of booty and spoils" (*caeca . . . incauta . . . / femineo praedae et spoliorum ardebat amore*, 781–2). Here is another sort of fire and love, but the deception and death that it leads to are familiar.

Her life departs with a groan to the shades below, just as Turnus' will. Inevitably the two are linked, both as victims of the war that has come to Italy.

Italy

At the beginning of Book VII the Trojans sail from Cumae up the coast to the mouth of the Tiber. They go with a calm breeze at night, on a sea that is bright with moonlight, but as they pass Circe's island (now Monte Circeo) they hear the roaring of chained lions and the raging of pigs, bears, and wolves, once men but changed into beasts by Circe's magic. It is as if the Trojans were putting behind them that part of the world Odysseus knew, not only Circe's "dire shores" (*litora dira*, 7.22) but other supernatural monsters (*monstra*, 21) as well, all that is inhuman, foreign, and terrifying.

But with the dawn, as always in the *Aeneid*, comes reality. The winds fall, leaving a dead calm, and Aeneas sees a "huge" grove, *ingentem lucum* (29), meaning rather (in Virgil's appropriation of the epithet) "native, natural, in the character of the place." The next lines are, I think, unique in Latin poetry – not a stylized *locus amoenus*, not a borrowed description of a rustic setting, but something that could only have been observed and felt on such a morning by Virgil himself: birds and birdsong in the lush growth of a river bank on a spring morning (32–4). This belongs with other passages of Virgil's own observation, such as the lengthening shadows on a mountain across a valley at sunset (*Ecl.* 1.82–3) or the light and "bristling" shadow of trees on a ridge line (*Aen.* 1.164–5). Aeneas enters the shaded mouth of the Tiber with gladness (*et laetus fluvio succedit opaco*, 7.36). He has left the wanderings of Odysseus behind him now. He is home.

We saw a similar naturalistic setting when, at the beginning of Book VIII, the waves and woods of the Tiber wonder at the "shields of men" and at Aeneas' warships, an unaccustomed sight. That was the problem for Virgil: a worthy foe had to oppose the Trojans in this Iliadic half of the poem, but

Virgil also conceived of Italy as a land of peace before the Trojan invasion, and that peace was an essential element in the character of the land. He did not try to find a logical solution to this contradiction, and as a poet he did not need to. The fascination is in watching how he maintains this impossible opposition.

Latinus is not only the king of Latium, but as his name suggests, is synonymous with it. "King Latinus, now old, was ruling the countryside and cities contented in a long-established peace" (7.45–6). This is our introduction to him, and we expect the traditional genealogy in the Homeric fashion – a father and grandfather at least, and perhaps ultimately a god. That is what we get, but with a significant difference. We learn (*accipimus*, 48 – the actual tradition varied) that his mother was a nymph and his father Faunus, a native and prophetic divinity of the woods. His grandfather was Picus – that is, a woodpecker. And his great-grandfather, the origin of the line (*ultimus auctor*, 49), was Saturn. There is not a trace here of warriors of any sort.

On the day after the arrival, Aeneas sends a hundred ambassadors to Latinus, while he himself makes ready for war, laying out the trench and walls for his camp. As they approach the towered walls (*augusta moenia*, 153; *turris*, 160) they find military exercises in progress (162–5).

There is a meeting in the palace of Picus, "august, huge, lofty with a hundred columns," a place filled with the awe and fear of the ancient spirits of the forests (*horrendum silvis et religione parentum*, 172) that was the earliest stratum that we can see of Roman religion. The space was then used for many purposes, a temple where the kings took office and the Senate met, and a hall for religious feasts (173–5). It was also a sort of museum, exhibiting a strange collection of portraits from the pacific and naturalistic past and as well the trophies and equipment of military history. There are the busts, fashioned from cedar, of ancestors – Italus, Sabinus (a cultivator of vines with his pruning knife), old Saturn himself, and Janus – and the other kings in order, "wounded in their country's wars" (182). There is armor, and captured chariots, axes, helmets, the bars of city gates, darts, shields, and (most anachronistic of all) the prows of ships (*rostra*). Lastly, there is Picus himself with civic emblems, "tamer of horses," but who was turned into a bird by Circe's love and magic (187–91). How many kings could there have been, who assumed power here, when there were only two generations between Saturn and Latinus? And what great cities were all these battles and naval engagements fought against, when pre-Saturnian Italy was a land of scattered, untaught, mountain peoples (8.321–2)? These, of course, are questions not to be asked. What we see in this museum is not history, but various and conflicting elements in the Latin character.

Latinus, in his speech of welcome, claims that the Latins are a just people, not because of laws and compulsion, but voluntarily, in the tradition of Saturn, their ancestor (*neve ignorate Latinos / Saturni gentem haud vinclo nec legibus aequam, / sponte sua veterisque dei se more tenentem,* 202–4). In Saturn's Golden Age there was no need for law or force. But though Latinus rules a country in peace, his city still has its walls and its youth training in military exercises. An agreement reached, Ilioneus gives Latinus tokens of Priam and Troy (243–8), and Latinus in return gives the ambassadors a hundred horses, all bedecked with purple and gold, plus a chariot with Circean horses for Aeneas (274–83) – significant gifts, of wealth and war.

The first cause of the war is Silvia's stag. Her name is obviously significant, and she is the sister of Tyrrhus, "whom the royal herds obey and to whom the guardianship of the fields, far and wide, is entrusted" (7.485–6) – in other words, he is a herdsman and his realm is the pastoral countryside. A marvelous stag has been raised from birth by the family, who adorn it with garlands, comb it, and wash it in a pure spring (483–9). This idyllic oneness of man and nature is furthered by a clear suggestion of golden age harmony: the stag, accustomed to human touch, fed at his master's table, after a day spent roaming the woodlands returns "home" at night, no matter how late (490–2 – for this conceit, see e.g. *Ecl.* 4.21–2).

Allecto seizes upon this opportunity to stir up the countryside after her success with Amata and Turnus, and she does so with little effort. She simply sets Ascanius' hunting dogs on the scent (475–81), and we then forget that she is there: the deed is made to appear entirely Ascanius' responsibility and due to his initiative. Indeed, he shoots the fateful arrow "aflame with desire for outstanding heroic praise," a phrase in which by this time every word is suggestive (*eximiae laudis succensus amore,* 496). Three transitional stages can be seen here: hunting has invaded the pastoral oneness with nature, and "the love of heroic renown" is in the process of transforming the weapons of the hunt into the weapons of war. The pattern is exactly that of Camilla's story.

The stag is shot as it floats downstream in a perfectly pastoral setting, "relieving the heat in the greenery of the river bank" (*fluvio cum forte secundo / deflueret ripaque aestus viridante levaret,* 494–5). The wounded deer is, of course, the imagistic focal point of Book IV. Dido burns with the fire and wound of love, like a deer pierced by the shaft of a hunting shepherd, who does not know he has hit his mark (4.68–73). How thoroughly the *Aeneid* is a single whole can be appreciated from this one example of the interplay of images: why the hunter of Dido's simile is a shepherd, and how this is significant in its application to Aeneas, can only be grasped from this event in the Latian countryside.

The violation of pastoral innocence brings an immediate reaction. The country folk arm with whatever weapons they happen to have at hand, rough staffs, clubs, axes, and the like – there is not a single spear in sight. "A fierce plague lurks silently in the woods" (*pestis enim tacitis latet aspera silvis*, 505): this plague is to be understood from the second half of *Georgics* III, where the pastoral landscape contained the sources of its own destruction – the snake, the gadfly, the fire of disease, all at home in the heat of the midday that is the essential quality of the pastoral world. Virgil sounds this theme here as an aside, but it is an important reminder: the peace of the pastoral world is only apparent, for the balance of its characteristic heat can at any time be upset, setting loose the sickness that hides within. The rustic brawl, fought with clubs and fire-hardened stakes, soon becomes a grain field of swords and bronze (*non iam certamine agresti / stipitibus duris agitur sudibusve praeustis, / sed ferro ancipiti decernunt atraque late / horrescit strictis seges ensibus*, 523–6).

There are two ways of thinking about the prehistory of man, which could be called the Cave and the Garden. The Cave is a scientific, anthropological approach, and the Garden mythological or religious. Each view has many possible variations, and since both are well known, only a quick review and reminder are necessary here to offer a concluding summary of Virgil's picture of pre-Trojan Italy.

The Garden, of course, in one of its manifestations is the Garden of Eden, where man begins in innocence in a setting of nature's sufficiency. No work is required (except by Milton), and since everything is there for the taking, there is no need for social organization of any sort, and laws, commerce, and war are unheard of. Man's character, then, is essentially good, and the inevitable decline that must follow is always due to some external cause, never to a flaw or fault within. Innate goodness is there from the beginning. In Greece Hesiod was the source of the Five Ages of Man, the decline from the Golden Age through Silver, Bronze, Heroes, and Iron (*Works and Days*, 106–201). The golden race of men lived in the time of Cronos (Saturn to the Romans) and knew neither struggle, woe, nor old age. They lived in peace and plenty on an earth that freely provided fruits and flocks. It is not until the Alexandrian poet Aratus that we hear again of the Five Ages. In the *Phaenomena* his description of the constellation Virgo tells of the maiden Astraea's happy association with the blessed mortals of the Golden Age of peace and plenty, when she was called "Dike" ("Justice"). She then had a much less happy time among the evils of the Silver Age, and her final

departure from the earth and men was the result of her loathing for the
race of bronze (96–136). The extraordinary and continuing popularity of
Aratus' astronomical poem at Rome, together with a Roman readiness
to see a decline in human affairs, meant for poets a new interest in the
Hesiodic Ages: it supplied them with a valued set of terms and images, not
for scientific explanation, but for poetic reflection.

The Greeks, as everyone knows, were thinkers, the discoverers of the
mind. Scientific anthropology had no use for such nonsense as the Five
Ages, which is why the Ages seem to have gone underground until Aratus.
Whereas the Garden assumes a decline from innocence and goodness, the
Cave is based, naturally enough, on progress, and progress always comes
from intellectual discovery. Man begins in a state no different from that of
the beasts, living in caves and subsisting as best he can on a miserable diet
of acorns and the like, with a bit of meat if he can kill it before it kills him.
Progress comes slowly, from the cave to rude huts, herds, agriculture, and
social organizations. Law is the crowning achievement of human society,
and commerce evolves in step with sailing, navigation, and the knowledge
of astronomy. "Many are the wonders, but nothing is more wonderful than
Man," sings the chorus in Sophocles' *Antigone* (332–75), listing the
achievements of civilization and the intellect.

This is the theorizing of Greek anthropologists such as Democritus,
readily available to Virgil's readers in the long account of Lucretius
(5.925–1457). (See also Juvenal's later and very amusing summation,
6.1–13.) But progress is not necessarily a good thing. Not only do we share
our origin and therefore our basic nature with the beasts, but the arts of
civilization, which follow from Prometheus' theft of divine fire, bring with
them a host of evils, ultimately and most notably war. The wealth and
luxury of modern cities are actually the symptoms of decline from a happy
state of primitive self-reliance, from the solid values still to be found on
the farm of our ancestors or among the peoples living in innocence far
from the demoralizing influences of civilization. And with this step we are
back to the Garden, but a scientific Garden, without its mythological or
religious orientation, inhabited now by the Happy Savage. Such thinking
is familiar to readers of Caesar on the Gauls and Germans, or of Tacitus (so
often) on Rome's decline.

How then does Virgil conceive of early Italy and its prehistory? The answer,
as always when Virgil touches upon something philosophical, is "inclu-
sively and eclectically," because he is a poet, not an anthropologist,
historian, or philosopher. A poet such as Virgil makes connections by gathering and arranging pieces and objects, through which we see the patterns
and conflicts of diverse elements in our world. He leaves to others the

business of the logical narrowing and excluding that arrives at a single answer, QED.

Evander, like a good tour guide, gives Aeneas a brief lecture on the history of Pallanteum before the actual tour starts (8.314–36). The original inhabitants were fauns and nymphs, and "a race of men born from the hard wood of oak trees" (a Homeric concept). They, of course, were without any of the hallmarks of civilization (*neque mos neque cultus*, 316) – no plowing, no storing of resources, no need to live thriftily – because the forest (*rami* – we can assume the oak and the arbute) and hunting sustained them. Evander is speaking here as an anthropologist, delivering a lecture on what we can call "primitivism." But then ("Next slide, please") something entirely different – the arrival of Saturn from Olympus, fleeing the weapons of Jupiter and exiled from his stolen kingdom. The Jovian takeover in the *Georgics* marked a crucial moment in world history, when man was forced to make his living by the sweat of his brow and the inventiveness of his intellect. Saturn's Latian refuge (*Latium . . . latuisset*, 322–3), though, was a period of the continued sufficiency of nature, but of a kind different from harsh primitivism: "What they call (*perhibent*) the golden ages (*aurea saecla*) existed under that king: thus he ruled his people in contented peace, until gradually came a worse age of baser hue, and the madness of war (*belli rabies*) and greed (*amor habendi*)" (324–7). *Perhibent*, as often, marks a footnote, obviously here citing Hesiod and Aratus. Evander then finishes his lecture as a proper prehistorian, with a catalogue of immigrant peoples (328–36).

One last passage calls for attention. In the last third of Book IX the Trojans are besieged within the walls of their camp, an occasion, though, for Ascanius to make his one appearance as a combatant. He kills one Numanus Remulus with a single arrow through the head. Virgil begins the incident by pointing out that previously Ascanius had used his weapons only as a hunter (*ante feras solitus terrere fugaces*, 9.591): he is making the critical transition from hunting to war, which by this time should make us somewhat uneasy. His victim, though, elicits little sympathy. Numanus taunts the Trojans for their eastern effeminacy, very much as had Iarbas in Book IV (215–17), contrasting their dress, sloth, and ecstatic worship of Cybele (9.614–20) with Italian hardiness. His taunts (Virgil says) are both deserved and undeserved (*digna atque indigna relatu*, 595), just as Rumor in Book IV mixes truth with lies (*[Fama] tam ficti pravique tenax quam nuntia veri . . . et pariter facta atque infecta canebat*, 4.188, 190). Numanus' Italians sound like Caesar's Germans (cf. *BG* 6.21.4–5 especially), and with good reason: both peoples are the exemplars of the sturdy virtues of societies untouched by the debilitating influences of civilization. The Italians are a hardened race (*durum a stirpe genus*, 603) inured to cold from birth (*natos . . . saevoque gelu duramus et undis*, 603–4), trained in hunting, enduring labor and content with little, for whom even agriculture is a military exercise. Warfare is their entire way of life, even in old age (603–13).

With this we have come a long way from those indications of the innate peacefulness of Italy with which we began. What is the truth in what Numanus says, and what is undeserved, unworthy to relate? Virgil never says, and he has no single view of pre-Trojan Italy. The character of the land and its people is a blended mixture of many elements, often opposing, but, as we come to know it, without contradiction. The Trojans bring war and an eastern decadence to a land of Saturnian peace, with its primitivistic harmony between man and nature, but Italy is also a land that produces a people with the hardness of oak and iron, a *durum genus*, whose life is war.

3

Fate and the Gods

First of all, we need to be clear that the *Aeneid* is not a poem about religion and that Virgil was not a philosopher.

Yet Fate and the gods are everywhere throughout the poem, seeming to be always in control. There is Jupiter, acting often as the agent of something that can be called Fate (the neuter *fatum* or its plural *fata*, etymologically "what was pronounced, uttered"), and there is his consort Juno, who, if she cannot change what is fated to be, can and does at least delay the process (as she says in her savage anger, 7.310–16). Virgil himself, in the proem, introduces his hero as "an exile by Fate's decree" and his epic as an almost Miltonic exploration – "Can such anger be in the minds of gods?" (1.2, 11). Is Jupiter himself subject to a predetermined universal order, or is he, though "ruler of gods and men," only its agent? Is human action preordained, and are men puppets whose strings the gods play with for their own amusement and gratification? Is it simply "fated" that Troy fall, that Aeneas leave Carthage, that Rome will rise? Do Venus and Juno control Dido and Aeneas, and does a grand destiny demand Dido and Turnus as sacrifices – pitiable, perhaps, or tragic, but necessary and justified? Such questions are only a beginning, and the discussion goes on without end.

But I repeat (yet again): Virgil was a poet, not a philosopher, moralist, or theologian. There are moments in the poem, certainly, when religious or philosophical concerns are suddenly there: there is, for example, the Numidian Iarbas, son of Jupiter Hammon, as the paradigm of the religious man who, like Job, is forced to question his faith, and there is Anchises in the Underworld lecturing on the purification and rebirth of souls. And there are, too, any number of lines which can be adduced as evidence of Stoic or Epicurean ideas, according to which the workings of Fate (and much else) can be systematically understood. Such "ideas," though, were the inevitable commonplaces, the necessary baggage, of the Roman mind, without which no communication or reflection was possible. For example, we could comb any work of modern fiction for terms, ideas, or icons that might themselves immediately be traceable to the Judeo-Christian tradition or to Freudian psychology, and yet no one would think of that work as a religious novel or a Freudian analysis. Virgil was neither Lucretius nor Milton. I am going to suggest in a few pages what I think Virgil is doing with these gods and with his great theme of destiny, knowing that a full argument is impossible here but hoping that I can offer some acceptable sense and clarity as a point of departure.

The Roman Gods

The first and most difficult step in an appreciation of the gods in Virgil's epic is to understand what the Romans felt their gods to be. We tend to see them as the gods we knew as children through the stories of Greek mythology, a varied set of divinities in charge of different spheres of activity – "X is the god of this, and Y of that" – whose good will and support could be obtained through sacrifice and prayer; and we naturally attribute to the Romans the beliefs and attitudes that we regard as essential to religion. In doing so, we get it all wrong.

The Romans had no religion. This statement is true if by "religion" we mean something like a set of beliefs that can be summed up in a creed, a moral obligation to live a just life, a personal responsibility to achieve our individual salvation, a spirituality that shows itself in fervent prayer and devotion, and a belief in a divinity whose blessing and grace we can hope to obtain through prayer or mystical communion. The Romans had none of this, and hence throughout the history of the city and empire they were always ready to accept with enthusiasm those various foreign cults that offered the mystery and fervor of a personal religious feeling: the Phrygian Magna Mater, the rites of Dionysus, the cult of Isis from Egypt, Mithraism, and finally Christianity. The state authorities regarded these foreign cults as serious threats which had to be opposed, suppressed, or rendered harmless through official appropriation.

The earliest Indo-European settlers of Latium seem in fact to have worshipped no gods at all, and this huge blank void persisted in the religious psyche of the Roman people throughout their history, an inherited subconscious disposition that might almost be viewed as genetic. Those pastoral settlers of the Palatine and Esquiline hills and their neighbors lived with the fear and dread of nameless, undefined spirits inhabiting places and objects around them – a forest or grove which could not be entered or cut without grave danger, or a stone once struck by lightning and thus possessing still a certain power, or a spring or stream with its indwelling spirit. This "animism" regards the natural world with fear and seeks to keep these spirits outside the boundaries of home and farm by established rites that have more to do with magic than with religion. What is the difference between religion and magic? At the risk of oversimplifying, we can say that the religious person makes a request for favor to a known and far superior deity through prayer, whereas magic attempts to bind, through words and acts, powers that are often unknowable in order to control them and force their co-operation. Much of what we know of early Roman ritual and formulaic prayer is the direct development from this original animism and is far closer to magic than what we would define as proper religion. *Religio*, a word almost always embarrassingly difficult to translate, etymologically means a "binding"; we always want to make it mean something it doesn't.

I can offer no details of this fascinating (to use a word of magical significance) area, except to call attention to one passage in Virgil's epic that shows clearly just how attuned Romans of his time still were to the spirit of animism centuries old. King Evander, receiving Aeneas at the site of Rome, has been offering his visitor a thoroughly anachronistic account of rite and custom, when the tour takes them by the foot of the Capitoline hill (8.347–54) – "golden now," says Virgil, "but then a place of shuddering fear, thickets of wild growth. Even then religious fear, the dread awe of the place (*religio . . . dira loci*), terrified the trembling country folk." Evander then tells Aeneas that a god inhabits this grove and hill, but it is not known (*incertum*) just what god it is. His words recall an old formula used to call upon an unknown spirit of a grove – "whether you be god or goddess" (*sive deus sive dea*, or *sive mas sive femina*). Reflective Romans were never out of touch with their first animistic experience.

This brief review is intended only to suggest just how late and psychologically superficial was the importation of the Greek Olympians. Before the beginning of the seventh century or thereabouts, the animistic spirits (*numina*) must have begun to acquire names and perhaps even some vague form. The wilderness of thicket and wood was now inhabited by something called Mavors, or Berber, or some similar name long lost. What seems particularly strange to us is the personification as deities of aspects of the farmer's life. The agricultural processes themselves came to be deified ("Plowing," "Harrowing," "Sowing," and others), and "Mildew" and "Good Harvest" became gods (*Robigus* and *Bonus Eventus*) along with others of the same sort: here too sympathetic magic was at work.

The impetus was there, then, for the first temples built at Rome. The fact that there were no earlier temples is in this context highly significant: they came from two sources, from Etruria just north of the Tiber, and from the Greek trading posts (*emporia*) and colonies south in Magna Graecia. The great temple of Jupiter Optimus Maximus on the Capitoline, alluded to in anticipation by Evander in the passage just mentioned, was in origin dedicated to the Etruscan triad of Jupiter, Juno, and Minerva, and was attributed by tradition to both Tarquins, the Etruscan kings. Rome's commercial center was just outside the city proper, downstream and on the left bank of the Tiber, where Santa Maria in Cosmedin is today, and was populated by Greek traders. The adjacent Aventine hill was the "Greek quarter" and plebeian too, and it was here that a temple of Diana was built (traditionally by Servius Tullius) and, at the beginning of the fifth century, a temple to Ceres, Liber, and Libera. In the Forum Boarium, the "cattle market" between the Aventine and the Tiber, was the Ara Maxima of Hercules, whose festival was being celebrated by Evander when Aeneas arrived; and nearby was the first temple at Rome to Apollo (431 BC). The Greek gods, then, came to Rome with Greek traders and were installed in their new quarters not by the ruling patricians, but, outside the city proper, by the people.

The temples which then began to be built inside the city tell a great deal about this later stage of Roman "religion." Here the state, meaning its patrician families, was in charge. On the Capitoline, looking down over the Forum, was Jupiter's old Etruscan temple, but he had now become a god of the state, the goal of the triumphal processions of Roman generals, for instance. Directly below, at the end of the Forum where the Senate met and the people voted, were the temples of Saturn and Concordia – the one a transformed personification of an early spirit of "Sowing," the other an abstraction like "Good Harvest." At the other end of the public area was the temple of the Dioscuri, Castor and Pollux – not quite gods, certainly not Olympians, but protective agents of the Roman army. And nearby was the shrine of Vesta, a personified public representative of another spirit, that of the hearth and its fire; its proximity to the Regia (originally the house of the king) speaks to the civic function of the cult.

It cannot be said that these and other gods were "worshipped," any more than the dread spirit of the woods just outside the protecting boundary stones of the farm was worshipped by the generations of farmers whose prayer (now addressed to a personification called "Mars") is recorded by the elder Cato. Just as this prayer is in fact a magical incantation, and the sacrifice that accompanied it still very much an act of sympathetic magic, so in the case of the civic gods who inhabit these recent temples we do not see worship as we know it, but rather acts performed by representatives of the state on behalf of the people. Participation in religious activity was entirely individual: the *paterfamilias* of Virgil's day still performed annual rituals that protected his family, just as the various priesthoods did for the protection of the state, but there was no collective worship, no truly religious enthusiasm shared by a group in the presence of the god: for that you had to go across the Tiber to the temple of Isis – foreign and very low class.

These Roman temples, too, speak clearly of what they are. Go to the great Greek temples of Sicily (which the Romans were well acquainted with from the time of the First Punic War) or just south of Naples to the archaic temples at Paestum, and you see just what a Greek temple was – a shaded colonnade, easily accessible by the three wide steps running all around it, an invitation to gather, stroll, and talk. Back home at Rome, though, the message was very different: look, be awed, but keep off, respectfully. Roman temples retain their Etruscan origin. They are typically built on massive, high podia, with many steps in the front only, steep and narrow, leading up to the cella; ritual is performed at the altar in front on ground level, as if the deity too, high above, were only an observer. The temple to Venus Genetrix, closing the far end of Julius Caesar's new Forum, makes a powerful statement, but its message is political. Nor was there any sense of worship or religious feeling to be derived from the temple to Divus Iulius built by Augustus to close the east end of the Roman Forum: its high podium, which could be used by spokesmen for the new order, looked directly across the length of the Forum (bounded on each side by the restored Julian basilicas) to the old *rostra*, the old area for public voting, and to the Julian Senate house. Finally, in Augustus' own Forum, the temple to Mars Ultor, with its flanking colonnades and hemicycles, is no more than a museum of Augustan iconography. The statements made by these three temples are powerful, but political, not religious.

We have seen little of the Olympians in this brief survey. In Cato's time (the first half of the second century) Mars could still be purely a spirit of the wilderness, though he had also, and for a long time, assumed the armor and the personality of Ares. The Diana of the Aventine, whether originally from Ephesus or from neighboring Aricia, assumed the attributes of the Artemis of Greek poetry. Apollo had to wait four centuries for a second temple at Rome, but when he finally acquired it (thanks to his overseeing Octavian's victory at Actium), he moved in comfortably with all his books and his war mementos too: he had become well known to Romans over those years as a literary gentleman and had no need of a Roman name.

The Olympian gods arrive in Rome after a long and difficult journey, finding homes in temples only slowly and late, and they come not so much as gods in any real sense, but most often as characters in Greek literature. Rome's first hexameter poet, Quintus Ennius (who died in 169), was able to fit the twelve Greek Olympians into two lines of the new verse: *Iuno,*

Vesta, Minerva, Ceres, Diana, Venus, Mars, / Mercurius, Iovis, Neptunus, Vulcanus, Apollo. It seemed a neat trick but, like all good tricks, the artfulness of it concealed its difficulty. A few years later (in 146) a Roman army captured Corinth, an event that came to stand for Rome's own ultimate surrender, as Horace famously had it: "The capture of Greece captured its fierce victor and brought the arts to rustic Latium" (*Graecia capta ferum victorem cepit et artis / intulit agresti Latio, Epist.* 2.1.156–7).

It is important to understand, then, that the gods in Virgil's epic are far from being the figures of religious awe or worship that we instinctively feel is due to divinity. For the average Roman, Jupiter would be primarily a representation of civic power, housed impressively in his temple on the Capitoline, but in no sense evoking homage or personal commitment. If in Virgil's epic he is so often "the father of gods and men," so he had been in Ennius' epic and in Homer's too; he can be simply a figure from poetry, inspiring neither religious nor nationalistic awe, and certainly not demanding "belief." The other major actors in the *Aeneid*, Juno and Venus, are similarly poised between their political duties and their literary (largely Homeric) roles. Juno had been the protector of Carthage, just as Virgil introduces her, and in fact, before the final destruction of that city in 146 BC, the Romans had actually performed a ritual, calling upon her to leave her temple and city and to come over to their side, thus absolving themselves in advance of possible desecration (again a rite of magic, we should note). But she can also be the jealous wife of Greek literature, her ever-popular comic role. Venus is the divine origin of both Rome and the Julian family, the Venus Genetrix of Julius' Forum, the mother of Aeneas, ever concerned for his descendents and the great city to come, and as such she is a purely political statement, and a powerful one. But she is also "golden Aphrodite," who in the *Iliad* only plays at war and, when wounded slightly by Diomedes, runs to Zeus for comfort; hence, she can be simply Jupiter's little girl, a suitably comic role to play against the petty jealousy of Juno as the wronged wife.

We have made three observations, which we can sum up before going on. (1) These Roman gods have little, if anything, to do with what we think of as religion. What survived of primitive animism could still be found in Virgil's day, but it had become, for the most part, a set of superstitions and formulaic magic. (2) The Greek Olympians were late comers, appropriated by the state so as to lose their foreign accents, whether Etruscan or Greek, as soon as possible, and were never that numerous a population when compared with the earlier settlers living in older housing (e.g., Mater Matuta, Janus, Concordia, Castor, Fortuna Huiusce Diei, and others – a mixed lot, and far more interesting). We should not deny the Olympians their share of power, however, when we deny them religious significance, but it is the power of symbolic abstraction, representing national aspirations, the glorious past, and pride in what must come: the iconography of Augustus' Forum was powerful and real, having the same sort of emotional impact on a Roman as a visit to the nation's capital has on an American today. (3) On the other hand, or at the other extreme, those Romans who knew their Homer, or had studied with the philosophers and rhetoricians in Athens during the equivalent of a college year abroad, knew perfectly well that the inherent rationality of the Greek mind could find much amusement in the Homeric gods: there was certainly enough irreverence in Homer to offend Plato. In any event, the Greek gods at Rome belong primarily to literature, to drama and poetry.

The Gods in the *Aeneid*

Virgil's gods exist in a state of tension between these two extremes of their reality outside of the poem – the political and the literary. What results from this tension is one of Virgil's great profundities, and one that is not theological or moral, but poetic.

The question of celestial anger is posed by Virgil at the end of the proem, and as the poem begins, it might seem that the anger of Juno has been set before us in the place of the wrath of Achilles. As Juno sees Aeneas' fleet setting sail from Sicily on the short leg to Italy, their journey nearly over, she is seized with an anger very similar to Achilles' anger in the first book of the *Iliad*: her rage is vented in purely heroic terms as she compares her own impotence to thwart fate and Trojan success to the simple ease with which Pallas Athene had blasted Ajax, son of Oileus, on his return from Troy. She, both sister and wife of Jupiter, is motivated by the archaic values of heroism – the honor that should follow from primacy: "Who now adores the divinity of Juno or in supplication will set honor on my altars?" (1.48–9).

She goes to Aeolus, in a scene not without touches of the comic in the subservience of Aeolus and his readiness to accede to sexual bribery. But the storm he releases is of extraordinary violence, universal and elemental: the sea gapes to reveal the earth beneath, fires flash in the upper air, and day becomes black night. Amid the cries of the men and the shrieking of wind in the rigging, with the immediacy of present death, we have our first sight of Aeneas, "his limbs loosed in cold fear," groaning and stretching his hands to the stars in prayer for the heroic death he could not have at Troy (1.92–101).

This is an extraordinary beginning and reveals much about what is to follow. Here is Juno, motivated as a Homeric hero, enraged at what she, like Achilles, perceives as violence done to her honor, appealing to Aeolus' basest instincts (his cupidity for social position and his sexual desire). The storm, though, is a paradigm of destructive violence loosed so easily by the loss of control, for Aeolus had been set by Jupiter himself to rule over and to keep in order these forces of anger, lest they sweep away and confound "seas and earth and high heaven" (1.56–63). The values of Homeric heroism, assumed by divinity, are transformed into a petty spitefulness that effects a sudden negation of universal order, of divinely imposed control over elemental violence. There, at the center of this violence, is a very human Aeneas, denied even the consolation of a hero's death.

As the epic comes to its close, Virgil has a similar, complementary scene of divine intervention. Book XII opens with Turnus under an intense and very strange light. His characteristic *violentia*, at the center of his conversation with Latinus, is developed in erotic language, and the subsequent scene with Amata and Lavinia is odder and more erotic still, as we saw in the previous chapter. The two champions then arm, like bulls about to fight (12.103–6 – a simile to be understood from a lengthy passage in the *Georgics*, 3.219–41, where two bulls fight over a beautiful heifer, illustrative of the all-consuming fire of sexual passion). The formalities preliminary to the single combat are begun. It is then that Juno, looking down from what will one day be called the Alban mountain, has second thoughts.

Even though she knows full well that the fateful day is at hand, she is no more than ever ready to yield, though she cannot herself bear to watch Turnus' defeat and death. She summons Juturna, Turnus' sister, who had been granted the honor of divinity after being ravished by Jupiter. Juturna is to act as Juno's surrogate: "Hurry, save your brother from death, if there is any way, or stir up war and confound the treaty. I will take the responsibility for this daring attempt" ('*auctor ego audendi*', 12.157–9). She then abandons Juturna, "uncertain and confused in her mind from this bitter wound" (*incertam et tristi turbatam vulnere mentis*, 160).

So begins this final, extended demonstration of divine cruelty in the *Aeneid*. What Juno sets in motion here is totally heartless. She knows, of course, what this day must bring, to the extent that she cannot even bring herself to be an observer, but such is the petty absorption in her own sense of being wronged that she will again bring confusion and slaughter upon the mortals gathered in ordered ceremony on the plain below. And Juturna, Turnus' own sister, whom Juno professes to love more than all her other rivals (142–5), is forced to act as the agent of this selfish cruelty.

Juturna, "confused and emotionally wounded," is the penultimate in a succession of human characters in the epic who are sacrificed to the demands of the heroic ideal and divine unconcern. She is human in the very fact of her blood relationship to Turnus, and as his sister she tries to save him from his inevitable death as a hero on the field. The divinity granted her by Jupiter in recompense for her virginity (141 and 878) turns out to be the cruelest of divine rewards, condemning her to an eternal separation from her brother, after his death (878–84). The final release from human suffering – the essence of "mortality" – is the condition of death, and this has been denied her (*'cur mortis adempta est / condicio?'*, 879–80).

If Juno acts with chilling cruelty here at the end, Jupiter outdoes her. We see different aspects of Jupiter throughout the epic – the concerned and slightly comic paternal figure consoling Venus; the ruler of gods and men, agent of destiny; and even, once, a movingly human deity who hears the grief and tears (*lacrimas . . . inanis*) of his son Hercules at the moment of Pallas' death and remembers his own sons, and especially Sarpedon, who fell at Troy (10.464–72). But the Jupiter that Virgil leaves us with, just like the final vision of Aeneas a few lines later, is terrifying.

There had to have been many ways (one would think) at Jupiter's disposal to remove Juturna from the scene. Why was it necessary to send one of the two Dirae? These are the Furies, as Virgil describes them (12.845–52), who attend the throne and threshold of "the savage king" (*saevi regis*), born from Night, sisters of the Underworld demon Megaera, winged and wreathed with coiling snakes. Their mission is to strike fear into wretched mortals (*mortalibus aegris*) "if ever the king of the gods moves dread death and sickness or terrifies deserving cities with war." Though unnamed here, they are Allecto and Tisiphone: the former had been sent by Juno in Book VII to rouse Amata, Turnus, and the countryside of Latium to war, an active personification of the madness of war; and she had appeared again as a savage participant in "the senseless anger" of battle (10.761). One of these two, sent by Jupiter, takes the form of a small owl, the bird of night, of dire omens, and of death (12.863–4), who flies repeatedly in Turnus' face and beats against his shield, "and a strange heaviness loosed his limbs in fear, his hair stood on end with horror, and his voice stuck in his throat" (865–8). Juturna recognizes the Fury and knows that she can do no more.

The pattern of divine action here at the end of the poem is very similar to Juno's participation at the beginning. In each instance the queen of the gods sends her surrogate to upset established order (in Book I Jupiter's control over the winds, and in Book XII the compact of peace between Latins and Trojans), and she does so for her own petty reasons, divinely oblivious to the mortal suffering that must ensue. Finally, we are left to reflect upon the willful cruelty of divinity – Juno's "mindful wrath," of course, but as well the cruelty of Jupiter, who, in sending the Fury, acts as "the savage king," setting in motion the terror of death, disease, and war (849–52). His influence is still in our minds and still to be felt on the battlefield just a few lines later, when Aeneas, "aflame with fury, terrible in his anger," kills Turnus (*furiis accensus et ira / terribilis*, 946–7).

These gods, then, are similar to Homer's gods, as Virgil frequently reminds us with his many parallels. They are actors in the epic world, differing from mortal actors only in that they lack mortality and thus cannot know sickness, age, or death. Virgil's gods, however, go beyond Homer's: they come to represent a certain unfeeling, careless malevolence that seems to be a necessary but inexplicable part of man's world.

Venus and Juno are very much involved in the tragedy of Dido, but to conclude that Dido dies simply because she has been controlled by these two goddesses, puppet-like, or has had to be sacrificed to some greater order, is to miss the real tragedy. As actors in the epic world, both Juno and Venus are primarily concerned, as we have seen, with their heroic honor. Juno's hatred of Troy and the Trojans results from a long series of slights that she feels she has suffered because of them. Venus' honor is entirely involved with Aeneas and the future of his line, the Julian family and Roman *imperium*. Like Caesar and Pompey, neither trusts the other, and with good reason.

The deception of Dido has its divine origin with Jupiter, when, having reassured Venus that Roman destiny remained unaltered, he sent Mercury to Carthage, "lest Dido, in ignorance of fate, refuse to receive the Trojans" (1.297–300). She is again deceived by divinity when, toward the end of Book I, Venus sends Cupid to take the place of Ascanius for one night, so that Cupid, embraced and fondly kissed by Dido, may "deceive [her] with trickery" (*falle dolo*, 1.684) and "inspire in her a hidden fire and deceive (*fallas*) her with poison" (687–8): "I am plotting," says Venus, always alert to and anticipating Juno's schemes, "to deceive the queen beforehand with trickery and to surround her with fire" (*quocirca capere ante dolis et cingere flamma / reginam meditor*, 673–4 – language that would be appropriate as well for the capture of Troy). Cupid's mission is "to kindle the queen's madness with gifts and plant the fire of love in her bones" (659–60), simply because of Venus' fear of Carthaginian treachery. Dido doesn't have a chance. When the two goddesses meet again, early in Book IV, Juno blasts her rival for having overcome Dido by this deceit and proposes her own resolution (a common kingdom), one that cannot be, as both goddesses know. A cynical agreement is reached, with obvious lack of commitment and trust on both sides, and "the Cytherean goddess laughs at this device of cunning" (*dolis risit Cytherea repertis*, 4.128). Laughter-loving Aphrodite had never before acted with such unconcerned cruelty.

This will be enough, I hope, to suggest what these gods are doing in Virgil's epic. It is usual to refer to "the divine machinery" of epic, as if the gods, or Fate, were in control of human affairs. Knowing what we do about Roman religion – what it was and (more important for us) what it was not – and realizing that these gods are figures of literature, we can assume, without clear indications to the contrary, that Virgil is not concerned with theological speculation, that he is not leading us in an exploration of the possibility of divine motivation in human affairs. It seems to me that Virgil was interested in the fact of Dido's love for Aeneas, that he thought about love as a fact, as something that often happens in human lives and that more often than not brings with it infatuation, pain, and even death, and is similar to other manifestations of madness (*furor*). He was not concerned, I think, with whether love was a good thing or a bad thing, or whether Dido or Aeneas might better have seen what was coming and taken steps to avoid it. Again, he was no moralist, but a poet.

If Virgil was primarily interested in the fact of human passion, and if the gods are not there for theological or moral reasons, what then is their poetic function? What, as Homeric figures who are human in every way except in their immortality, do they actually do? We must see them, I think, as actors, not as representations or abstractions. As actors they are showing us something that we can easily miss if we think of them as somehow representing religious or moral values, or serving as abstractions of superhuman power. This is not to deny that Jupiter, for instance, was often such a representation or abstraction for the Romans. He was, of course: that precisely was the daily import of his Capitoline temple, dominating the city, and that was his function supremely in Horace's great Roman Odes (*Odes* 3.1–6). Virgil's Jupiter, "who rules the affairs of men and gods with eternal power and who terrifies with his lightning blast" (to use Venus' grand formula of address, 1.229–30), can never be far removed from the representation of the *imperium* of the Roman state, and we are continually reminded of Jupiter as the great abstraction of supreme power, of order, of control over chaos and confusion.

But what always concerned Virgil was how all of our attempts to find or impose order, whether imaginative or intellectual, ultimately fail because of our very humanity, the irrepressible *furor* that marks our mortality. "Love has power over all: we too must yield to Love" (*'omnia vincit Amor: et nos cedamus Amori'*, *Ecl.* 10.69) is Gallus' ultimatum in the *Eclogues* – a poetic ultimatum that reverberates within us more powerfully than any message that logical discourse could devise. If the poetic imagination cannot create an ordered landscape capable of withstanding the *dementia* of human passion, neither can the scientific understanding of the *Georgics* ultimately control the reality of our physical universe: Orpheus –

magician and singer, who charms and controls even the power of death –
yields in one terrible instant to human *furor*.

When Virgil, then, came to epic and began to think of power and order
willed and created by man through time, through history and specifically
Roman history, what better way could he have devised to show how pure
power and control function – "pure" because not adulterated or contami-
nated by human weakness or failure – than through the actions of those
Homeric gods who do not know sickness, age, or death. The gods act, motivated by human passions, ambitions, and values (even by Homer's heroic
values, quite often), but the consequences of divine action – "pure" action
– fall upon those mortals who live in the real world of struggle and death
below.

Review, quickly, that perfect beginning to the poem. We have heard in
the proem of divine anger as the poet's subject, not Achilles' wrath, but
Juno's (pure anger, that is). Before we meet the human actors, we meet
Juno, acting (not unlike Achilles) from a bitter sense of wounded pride. Her
pride is far purer than Achilles', in fact, because it is totally without his
heroic nobility. She appeals to Aeolus' basest, though very human,
instincts. Jupiter's order, imposed over the discordant violence of the
winds, is upset and chaos results, not the sort of chaos that can be seen
on our human level, but an elemental and universal storm. And at the
height of its rage we finally meet Aeneas, praying for a death he was not
allowed to have, the victim of Juno's anger.

Divine action, then, is human action in a pure state, a purity of absolute
pettiness, of ambition and greed, of spite and pride; but pure also in that
it need have no regard for its consequences. When Virgil shows us the consequences, then, as he does in Aeneas' first desperate prayer, we see them
more clearly and experience them more deeply, since they follow, so often,
from this purer ether of divine action.

We have just committed the inevitable error, though: as we try to say
what Virgil *means*, reducing his poetry to the language of discourse, we
simplify and distort. When we focus on the human pettiness of the gods,
we ignore their essential grandeur. When we read of Jupiter, we must
remember those moments of solemnity in the *Iliad* when the will of Zeus
is to be felt with awe and terror, and we must remember the Capitoline
Jupiter at Rome. Virgil is never simplistic, and there are moments when his
gods know human suffering too. Jupiter can respond to Hercules' tears for
Pallas' death with a father's understanding and compassion (10.464–72)
and can recognize mortality: "To each there is a fixed day, for all a short
span of life without recall" (*'stat sua cuique dies, breve et inreparabile
tempus / omnibus est vitae'*). But having said these words, he then "casts
his gaze away from the fields of the Rutulians," becoming again the remote

observer, the immortal. In the Virgilian gods we *see* what is most human – anger, the pettiness of ambition, tears and sympathy – set before us in the clarity of the air of Olympus. It is their remote grandeur that makes what is human in their actions so terrifying.

When, at the end of the poem, Jupiter becomes the *saevus rex* and sends the Fury to terrify Turnus, we must still hold in our minds the almighty father (*pater omnipotens*) who restrains those universal forces of violence represented by the storm winds (1.60–3), imposing order and control with his "fixed compact" (*foedere certo*). The "savage king" who sends disease, war, and death to "wretched mortals" is this same universal ruler, as Juturna, yet another victim of divine deception, pathetically reminds us: "Nor does it escape me – I am not deceived – that these are the arrogant commands of great-spirited Jupiter" (*nec fallunt iussa superba / magnanimi Iovis*, 12.877–8).

In closing, let us take one more look at Venus. By the time we have finished Book I we have gotten to know her well. As a divine actor, she is motivated by pure ambition, unalloyed by any other human emotion or by any awareness of mortality. The suffering of her son means nothing to her, even at his lowest point of despair, when she meets with him on the Libyan shore – the occasion of his bitter words to her, "Why so often do you make sport of your son with deceptive images?" (1.407–8). She will do everything to assure his safety and survival, but only because he is necessary to her glorious future. We see her with Aeneas twice again, once (as he relates it) when he had just witnessed Priam's slaughter, and again when she delivers Vulcan's armor. At Troy (2.589–93) she appeared "such and so great as she usually appeared to the gods," bathed in pure light, just as Aeneas saw her turning away from him at Carthage; but she at least takes him by the hand, calls him "son," and tells him to flee, having revealed to him the gods engaged in Troy's destruction. So too, when she comes with the armor, she is the "shining goddess amidst the ethereal clouds" (8.608), but she "seeks the embrace of her son" (8.615). Are there indications here of some motherly affection, after all? Or is it more cruel deception? The gifts she brings are aflame with the fire of war and worked with the images of Rome's future. Aeneas seems important to her only as a delicate pivot on which depends the transition from Troy to Rome.

This is a mother who can bring upon her son, without the slightest concern, the desperate grief that he will feel on leaving Dido and realizing that he was the cause of her death. Even the purity of Juno's divine anger or of Jupiter's divine power (even as they both employ the Furies Allecto and Tisiphone in their service) does not come near the chilling perfection of Venus' inhuman indifference.

Fate in the *Aeneid*

What about Fate, then? It seems to be everywhere in the epic, a force that is as powerful as the gods or perhaps even more powerful, driving the human characters with a fixed necessity to a predetermined end.

How uninteresting this poem, or any poem or drama, would be if human events simply followed a predestined course. If it were supposed that a character knew what the course of events would be, then he would either go along with it, boringly, or could take arms against it, heroically, and fall opposing it, dumbly. This is often what we find in second-rate literature, but it is not the stuff of real heroic or tragic action. In good literature, Fate and inevitability are not the same thing. If all that happened to Oedipus were simply a matter of a preordained, unbreakable chain of events (Fate), who would really care? What is compelling in the play is his heroic determination to discover the truth about who he is, even as we know at every step what this, inevitably, will lead to. Romeo and Juliet may be "star-crossed lovers," but it is not the fact of their fated end that compels us, but rather how their love and innocence, opposed and thwarted by indifference and stupidity, take them inevitably to the final scene. It is the conflict that is important, not the inescapable end itself. "Fate" is often nothing but a shorthand, the code word, for what we know is going to happen. What happens in the *Aeneid* is not governed by a grand necessity: Virgil was not as boring as many of his interpreters.

Fate and free will were, of course, important concerns for Roman thinkers – that cannot be denied or ignored. The two major schools of philosophy at Rome (the Epicureans and the Stoics) differed essentially in their view of predestination, whether events (as the Epicureans thought) in the atomistic universe were the result of blind chance, or whether a Stoic divine mind exercised an ultimate control. The real problem is always how to avoid an absolutely mechanical, clockwork world. Few would want to deny to man a will of his own: without choice, life is both meaningless and uninteresting. For the unphilosophical man in the Roman street, seers of various sorts and astrologers especially could provide insight into what must be, inevitably, since if the future is knowable, it must be already fixed and in place, like the movement of the planets through the constellations of the Zodiac. Yet it is always interesting to watch astrologers, then and now, begin with the premise that knowing the stars only allows us to take advantage of certain conditions, to maximize opportunity and to minimize risk: seldom is a claim made for a completely mechanistic universe and an unavoidable destiny.

This is simply to suggest that when we meet with Fate in the *Aeneid*, even when Jupiter appears as its divine agent, we are in no way obliged to see the machinery of the universe at work, impassively grinding up unhappy mortals in its gears and wheels. Fate is an intellectual commonplace and in itself need not suggest any particular context of ideas – Stoic, say, or astrological. As we said at the beginning of this chapter, "Fate" is one of those ideas that belong to the common intellectual baggage that every Roman carried. Our tendency, when we meet it, is to assume that it must bring with it the whole Stoic (say) system, that the person using the term must be speaking as a philosopher of a particular sect. Here we have to be very cautious, remembering that we all use terms all the time that might seem to an observer two thousand years from now to be Freudian or Judeo-Christian (our intellectual baggage). When we see "Love" on a Valentine's Day card, we do not think of Christian *agape* or Freudian *eros*.

Most of the occurrences of *fatum* or its plural *fata* in the *Aeneid* mean simply "death." When Aeneas, in recounting the fall of Troy, says to Dido, "Perhaps you might ask what was Priam's fate" (*fata*, 2.506), he is certainly not inviting her to engage in postprandial speculation on predestination. "Fate" can also denote simply what has happened or what is happening, as when Dido, "terrified by fate" (*fatis exterrita*, 4.450), prays for death. She knows what has happened, that Aeneas is preparing for departure, and she sees dire omens of things to come: all this experience is there in the word "fate." Otherwise, fate is commonly associated with the destiny of individuals or of Rome. In either case, it can be a powerful poetic shorthand denoting what *we* know is going to happen – which is not at all the same as saying what was predestined to happen or preordained, divinely or mechanistically. But, just as the divine actors in the epic show us a pure perfection (whether of savage hatred, or of power, or of ambition) without consequence for themselves and therefore without their own responsibility, so Fate shows us the course of human events on a chillingly impersonal plane. We think of "the gods and fate" together in the *Aeneid* with good reason. Both can be expressions of universal indifference: what happens to "wretched mortals" doesn't really matter.

Let us return once again to Mercury's mission to Dido in Book I, when he is sent by Jupiter to assure her ignorance of fate. She is not to know what will happen to her personally, but, after what we have just heard from Jupiter about Rome's fate ("Spare your fear, Cytherea, the fate of your people remains unshaken," 1.257–8), the fate of which she is to be kept in ignorance of is Rome's great destiny. Her ignorance of what is to be is a fact of human existence. The great plan will go forward, as we know in fact it did. Somewhere, completely apart, there exist Jupiter, Venus, and an order of events that will happen, that we know has happened; elsewhere there is human ignorance and fallibility, and to the divine order Dido really doesn't matter at all.

Fate in the *Aeneid* is simply what happened – not what *had* to happen. It is a fact or a series of facts, not a force and not a philosophical concept. There are things that happen: someone, crossing a street just as he does every day, is hit by a bus; someone else suddenly develops a headache and is dead within a week. Perhaps reasons of a sort can be found for these events. There might have been a moment of inadvertence on the part of the pedestrian or of the bus driver, and in either case that moment might have an obvious explanation, which in turn could be more fully understood; and pathologists can explain the development of tumors. But for most of us, reacting to such events, the question is always "Why did it have to happen?", and to this question the last thing we expect is an answer.

Virgil was interested simply in the fact of what happened. We (Virgil's readers) know what happened because we know the history of Rome. We know (though these are only images) what Jupiter told Venus, what Anchises showed Aeneas, and what was on Vulcan's shield. Whether all this *had* to happen, Virgil doesn't care (though I suspect he would have thought the idea of a fixed, preordained destiny rather silly, or boring). What concerned Virgil was the human being at the center of this series of events, who cannot know anything at all about what has happened in the history that we know about.

Ignorance is fundamental to the human condition in Virgil's poem. All of Virgil's human characters are, necessarily, ignorant of what is to come, just as they are deceived by the images of the past that they have created and live by. Aeneas can never know what is to be, as Virgil makes clear by Aeneas' departure from the Underworld through the gate of false dreams and by his reception of the shield in dumb wonderment, "ignorant of history, rejoicing in its images." As the hero of this poem, though, he must participate in this process of history, or Fate, or simply of what happened. He does not know, for instance, why Creusa became separated from him on those dark streets as they fled from the fires of Troy, nor does Virgil himself offer the slightest sign of interest in why it so happened: all Aeneas knows is that it *did* happen and that he saw "nothing more cruel in the destruction of the city" (2.746). Fate is what happened, the senseless cruelty of the process of history.

Past and future are all that exist, and both exist only as images, unattainable and deceptive. Virgil's gods and Fate are sometimes agents, sometimes expressions, of this complex of images, with an emotional power and depth that only poetry is capable of. The human actors in Virgil's epic must necessarily be part of, and subject to, this temporal process, to history, which they cannot understand and which cares not at all for them, wretched mortals with aspirations to the heroic. It is time now to look at these images of past and future.

4

Virgil's Troy

There is not one Troy in the *Aeneid*, but many. There was first of all the Troy of Homer that all Romans for a long time had grown up with; the stories and heroes of Troy were familiar in a variety of ways even to those who knew no Greek. Then there was the city of the Julian family, from which at its fall the Aeneas of legend had fled with his son Ascanius, also, conveniently, known as Iulus; when Caesar built his Forum adjoining the Roman Forum, he installed Venus in a dominating temple at one end of it, in her aspect as Genetrix, the ultimate parent not only of the Trojan Aeneas and of the *gens Iulia*, but of the Roman people as well. In the *Aeneid*, the fall of Troy is the subject of Book II, and a major panel of Book III is set in Andromache's Troy, a restoration of the original. Aeneas is often seen in Trojan dress or with a Trojan entourage, and we are frequently reminded that this is a Trojan hero. While there are a finite number of references to or suggestions of Troy that could all be collected, catalogued, and described, no suggestion occurs in isolation but rather each brings with it overtones of other lines and passages, heard or half-heard in the reader's mind: hence the number of Troys in the poem becomes infinite, and the possibility of a reasoned catalogue becomes an exercise in scholarly futility.

In the *Aeneid* Troy is the past – Aeneas' past, and Rome's, and the reader's. What sort of a past does Virgil construct, for his hero and for us?

The Roman Troy

When Troy fell to the Greeks in 1184, a few Trojans managed to escape. This date was established by the Alexandrian polymath Eratosthenes and was accepted (as we will need to know shortly) as fixed and certain by the early Roman historians. (It has since proved to be surprisingly accurate.) A number of towns in Greece, Sicily, and Italy claimed to have been founded by Trojan exiles, according to local legends, and in Latium itself there appears to have been a hero cult of Aeneas at Lavinium, associated with the legend of his death in the river Numicus. His literary escape from Troy is as old as the Greek epic cycle and (probably) Stesichorus, the sixth-century lyric poet. By the third century BC, in any case, as the Romans began to write their own history almost *de nihilo*, Aeneas and his Trojans had become a fixed and important part of the city's prehistory.

These first historians worked with a canvas that was, for the period between Aeneas and the first kings, almost entirely blank. There was, for instance, a considerable variation in the dates given by these first historians for the actual founding of the city by Romulus, from as early as 900 to as late as 728 BC. The date that we view as traditional, 753 BC, was not established and accepted until 47 BC, on the authority of Varro, the greatest antiquarian scholar of his time, but it was entirely his invention. He arrived at it by a simple calculation: the first real date in Roman history was 509 BC, the beginning of the Republic and the consulship (though some modern historians have doubted both the date and what "the beginning of the Republic" actually signified), and working back from this, through the traditional seven kings with an arbitrary average reign of 35 years each, Varro reached 753. Clearly, there is no reality to this date at all. But there still remained a great deal of empty space in the historical canvas that needed filling in. Since Rome already had an eponymous founder in the legendary Romulus, and since 753 was over four centuries after Aeneas' arrival, how was this intervening period to be explained, and what was Aeneas actually doing in this picture?

Happily, someone discovered, or invented, the long rule of the kings at Alba Longa, and everything began to fall into place. Aeneas himself founded Lavinium, and lived there with his wife Lavinia (who some said was the mother of Ascanius) for three years, according to Virgil and Jupiter (1.261–74). Ascanius, also known as Iulus, then, after 30 years of rule, founded Alba Longa in the hills to the east. Then came the 300 years of the Alban kings, until the birth of Romulus and Remus and the fratricidal founding of Rome. All this adds up to 333, a very fine figure indeed, but it doesn't begin to get us to Varro's date of 753 for the founding: 1184 (the fall of Troy) plus the 7 years of wandering plus 333 gives us 844 for Rome's foundation. Clearly, chronological accuracy or even consistency was of no concern for either Virgil or his readers.

Romulus and Remus were the children of Rhea Silvia, the daughter of Numitor, the last Alban king, who had at this time been driven out by his younger brother Amulius. Their father (so she claimed to skeptics) was

Mars, who had raped her in spite of her having been made a Vestal (and therefore doomed to be childless forever) by Amulius. Rhea Silvia also had the good fortune, like Ascanius, of having another name, Ilia. How the babes grew up to found Rome is a story known to all.

Rome, then, could claim two founders: the Trojan Aeneas, son of Venus, and Romulus, son of Mars. The Julian family claimed the same descent. They were originally from Alba Longa, they said, coming to Rome at the time of Alba's destruction at the hands of Rome's third king, Tullus Hostilius. All this was ready at hand as Gaius Julius Caesar was establishing himself first as a leading contender and finally as the sole power at Rome. Just as his *Commentaries* provide a justification for his actions as a general in Gaul for eight years and then during the civil wars, on the grounds that he had only acted in the best interests of Rome, so he could present himself and the Roman people as, genealogically, one and the same. Thus Venus Genetrix came into her temple in his new Forum, from whom "the sons of Aeneas were descended" (as Lucretius had begun his Epicurean poem, published in 55, with the invocation to Venus, *Aeneadum genetrix*). Only a few details required tweaking, such as that Ascanius was actually called Iulus, and had been known at Troy as Ilus, and was in fact the son of the Trojan Creusa and not the Latin Lavinia, and that Rhea Silvia was known as Ilia. The Julians wanted to get the record straight on these and similar points. It did not make a bit of difference that *Iulus* is trisyllabic and begins with a short vowel, whereas the family name *Iulius* begins with the semivowel (Julius, as we spell it). The case for the connection would come to be made by no less of an authority than Jupiter himself: "Julius, a name descended from great Iulus" (*Iulius, a magno demissum nomen Iulo*, 1.288 – the only occurrence of the family name in the entire poem).

Aeneas' flight from Troy, with his father Anchises, his son Ascanius, and his household gods, had been represented on Greek vases and was to become a repeated scene on Roman coins, recalling again the common origin of the Julian family and the Roman people. Here, in one figure, are summed up the various aspects of *pietas*. "Piety" is the fulfillment of one's obligations to family, country, and gods. *Pius* is a frequent epithet of Aeneas throughout, seeming to be in the Homeric manner, but there is nothing formulaic about it: it does not occur casually. We must be careful not to bring to it any of our connotations of "piety." We must keep in mind, as we encounter the "pious" hero, that there is nothing in the Roman concept that suggests religious or spiritual devotion, no sense of moral or ethical rightness. *Pietas* means "duty," plain and simple. At the risk of trivializing, we might see it as joining the PTA, paying one's taxes fully, and attending church every Sunday: these are obligations, to family, state, and

God, but they do not necessarily have anything to do with moral, ethical, or religious values. Furthermore, we must also remember that *pietas* and *pius* should always recall the scene of Aeneas leaving Troy, beginning the journey to Italy, the hero doing what he must do, and not a man wrestling with questions of what is right or just, not a man of deep convictions and beliefs. For Aeneas, *pietas* is getting on with the mission, for the Julian family and for Rome.

The ancestors of the Romans were, as Indo-Europeans, rather odd: they seem to have brought with them into Italy no gods and no mythology, as we saw in the previous chapter. We could also say that in Italy they had no past. That vast blank on the historical canvas, that stretch of time between Aeneas and Romulus that had to be filled in, is eloquent evidence of this; and even the period of the seven kings, while the shadows of real history begin to be discernible, contains more fiction than solid fact. Roman historical reality begins with the stories of the great men preserved by the aristocratic families from the beginning of the Republic, until finally in the third century historical writing and "research" begin and historians, both Greek and Roman, start to fill in the blank areas. This stands in sharp contrast to the Greeks, for whom the sense of a real past, going back to the founders and first rulers of cities and even to heroes and gods, was to be felt every day, in the temples, streets, and fountains from agora to acropolis. In contrast, Rome was young, and in this was not unlike the American experience, when our relatively short history is compared with the historical richness of Europe. Just contrast Boston or Washington DC, two American cities rich in visible history, with the 3,000 years of the tangible past in Rome today. As soon as Rome began to play an important role in the Mediterranean, it needed to establish its past, and it was free to invent as much as it wanted.

For the ancient Romans, Troy provided an emotional antiquity. In their descent from the Trojan Aeneas, son of Venus, they made a connection with the Homeric world of heroes and gods: all this was now readily available for a people who were trying to construct a more recent, Italian past for themselves from the legends handed down by a few aristocratic families and from the half-forgotten stories connected with a few topographical monuments. Troy had a further advantage: it was not Greek, but rather the valiant opponent of the united Greek cities. The mythological, legendary, and divine resources of the Homeric world became part of the Roman past without that heavy feeling of inferiority to Hellenic history and culture.

But did any Roman actually believe in all of this? Did anyone of sense or education really think that his city began with the fall of Troy, or that Julius Caesar was a direct descendent of Venus – through the Vestal Ilia, through the kings of Alba Longa, and back to Iulus and Aeneas? Intellectually, probably no one did, at least literally, though fundamentalists are always to be found. We must approach such questions with an understanding that we live our collective lives symbolically, responding not to rational argument but to icons and pure symbols. Our political campaigns make this clear. We must have flags (and the more of them, and bigger, the better) as the backdrop for emotional speeches that are loaded with the icons of progress and prosperity, with the images of security and peace, with the symbols of the solid values that no one can oppose, and with references to the symbolic heroes of our national histories – Lincoln, Nelson, Garibaldi. Religious symbols are the most powerful we live with: even agnostics with a Judeo-Christian background react at some deep and instinctive level to a crucifix or the star of David, for these carry a huge weight of historical associations as well as purely religious ones. There are few true believers who read their scriptures without a suspension of the rational faculties, who would claim belief in the literal truth of every word and story, or who accept intellectually every tenet of a creed or every detail of ritual.

We need these national symbols and icons of an invented past, these powerful images that have no literal truth or reality. Troy provided the Romans with a meaningful set. "Did they actually believe that . . . ?" is a naïve question. Of course they did, just as we do, when we burn a flag or react with outrage to such a desecration. Augustus' temple to Apollo on the Palatine, splendidly rising next to the pretended simplicity of his own house, spoke clearly and daily to what Actium meant and to the humility of the new leader. Earlier, before Philippi, he had vowed a temple to Mars Ultor (Mars the Avenger), which was not finally completed and dedicated until 2 BC, 17 years after Virgil's death. The temple stood, rising high on its podium, at the far end of the new Forum Augustus had built adjoining Caesar's Forum, in which stood the smaller temple of Venus the ancestor: here was Mars, who had settled the score. The iconography of this Augustan Forum postdates the *Aeneid* (as we must always remember), but it is a splendid summary of what Roman Troy had come to stand for.

From the old Roman Forum, passing through Julius' Forum with its temple to Venus Genetrix, and entering Augustus' Forum, one saw at the far end, against a huge wall that blocked off the jumble of buildings behind and thus enclosed the space, the great temple. A portico ran down each side of the Forum itself, with small niches set into each rear wall containing the statues, with *tituli*, of the *summi viri*, a parade of the great men of Roman history. As one walked down one of these porticoes, toward the temple, two large hemicycles (*exedrae*) came into view, balancing each other, set on an axis with the front of the temple. At the center (rear) of the one on the left was Aeneas with his father, son, and the household gods,

fleeing Troy on that night of defeat; in the other *exedra* on the right, facing
the Aeneas group, was Romulus in triumph: *pietas* in defeat, *virtus* in
victory. Sharing the hemicycle with Aeneas were figures of the kings of Alba
Longa and the Julii; with Romulus, others of Rome's *summi viri*.

Moving back a bit, looking up – way up – at the pediment of the temple
itself one saw a whole history of the city, from its Trojan origin down to the
present. In the center of the pediment was Mars, the avenger of Julius'
assassination, in victory like his son Romulus as *triumphator* in the *exedra*
below. To the viewer's right – on the Romulean side, that is – were the
statues of Fortuna, then Rome (seated), and the Tiber (reclining in the
angle – the river where the twins had been found by the she-wolf). To
the left (the Trojan side) were Venus, Romulus (seated – and now associated with his ancestors the Alban kings and with Ilia and the Julii, all in the
exedra on the left), and the Palatine (reclining – the hill of Romulus' hut
and on which Augustus himself now lived).

Inside and at the rear of the temple was the cult statue of Mars, flanked
by Venus and the avenged Julius.

But all of this history of Rome, from Venus and Mars, Aeneas and
Romulus, and down through the *summi viri* to Julius, was focused on one
man, Augustus himself. In the center of the Forum area was the triumphal
four-horse chariot (*quadriga*) that the Senate and People had erected in
Augustus' honor when the Forum was finally dedicated in 2 BC, together
with an inscription listing all his victories, headed by the title *Pater Patriae*,
decreed at the same time.

Here, then, are the powerful images of divinity, nation, and family that
go back to the Roman Troy, a monument to Augustan *pietas*. All of Rome's
past was visible, and all of Roman history was there, leading ultimately to
the victory of one man: from Aeneas to Romulus to Augustus, the story of
duty and eventual triumph.

The Destruction of Troy (*Aeneid*, Book II)

Troy is Rome's origin as a nation, and it is the city of Homer and Homeric
heroism. It is also Aeneas' home. His account in Book II of its last night is
far more than a good story told after a good dinner. He tells of the personal
loss that is always and inevitably our individual past.

The structure of the book, as is always so with Virgil, tells us much. There
is a brief introduction (1–13) as Aeneas begins, very much like an epic
proem, and there is a brief conclusion (796–804) as the wretched gathering of exiles (*miserabile vulgus*, 798) set forth in the dawn of a new day.
Aeneas prepares his audience for a story he can hardly bear to relate, of

the unspeakable pain, tears, and grief of the final struggle of his city. Night has fallen at Carthage, and the eternal movement of the stars urge sleep – that is, the forgetfulness of mortal suffering (to paraphrase one of the most beautiful lines in Latin poetry, *et iam nox umida caelo / praecipitat suadentque cadentia sidera somnos*, 2.8–9). It is important to realize that the story is being told at night (night and day are always to be observed in this poem), because it concerns the events of a night of blindness and deception. Aeneas himself gives a summary of the structure of his narrative, "how the Danaans overthrew the wealth of Troy and a people of sorrow, and what I myself *saw*, and the great part I *played*." This is the tripartite division of the book: first how Sinon deceived the Trojans (13–249), then what Aeneas saw as Priam's city was being destroyed (250–633), and finally what he himself then did (634–795). In the first panel, he never once refers to himself, either as a spectator or as an actor; in the second, he is almost entirely a passive witness to what takes place; only in the third, after Troy has fallen and is no more, does he actually present himself as having an active role.

We can take this a bit further. Aeneas' narrative of Sinon's deception, so objective that it is easy to forget as we read that Aeneas is telling the story, tells of events that happen in the full light of day, a day, moreover, of misguided celebration, that is to be their last (*nos delubra deum miseri, quibus ultimus esset / ille dies, festa velamus fronde per urbem*, 248–9). Heaven turns, and that last day is followed immediately by night, rushing on from Ocean with Homeric solemnity, hiding in obscurity heaven, earth, and Greek deceit (*Vertitur interea caelum et ruit Oceano nox / involvens umbra magna terramque polumque / Myrmidonumque dolos*, 250–2). We have moved from day and human deception to the universal deception of night, as Aeneas witnesses the actual fall of his city. Finally, as fires burn everywhere, Venus for a moment removes the blindness of mortal vision to show her son the gods participating in the destruction: it is all over, and he returns home, after this moment of true revelation, to become an actor in the continuing blindness of this night. Let us now take a closer look at each of these three panels.

Throughout the first panel the theme of deception occurs again and again, from the very first rumor (*fama*, 17) that the Greeks have left, feigning (*simulant*, 17) that the horse is an offering for their safe return, to the finality of the city's fall, not because of Diomedes or Achilles, after ten years and a thousand ships, but because, blinded by pity, the Trojans believed Sinon's artful perjury (195–8). They are deceived precisely because, having now suffered through these ten years, they feel a human sympathy for Sinon. He concludes his story with a plea to Priam for pity (*miserere laborum / tantorum, miserere animi non digna ferentis*, 143–4), which is immediately and spontaneously offered (*his lacrimis vitam damus et mis-erescimus ultro*, 145). We remember Dido's reception of the Trojans near the end of the preceding book, "Knowing suffering myself, I have learned how to help the distressed" (*non ignara mali miseris succurrere disco*, 1.630). Pity is a rare quality in the ancient world, especially in the world of heroes: what results from human sympathy, for the Trojans here and for Dido later, is worth reflection.

Sympathy for human suffering, misplaced trust, and blinding deception all occur in the clear light of what was thought to be the first day of relief and peace. In this first panel and throughout the book these themes are recalled through the imagery of the serpent and the flame, a rich and complex association of suggestions that occurs often through language alone. For example, the real serpents that come for Laocoon and his sons flash fire from their eyes, and their tongues lick like flames (210–11). They come "sinuously" (*sinuat*, 208), and after them fear "insinuates" itself through the people (*insinuat*, 229): the Latin verb is specific for the coiling and writhing of snakes, and its connection with *Sinon* is inevitable. The horse, then, slithers into the city on "the glidings of wheels" (*rotarum . . . lapsus*, 235–6, and *inlabitur urbi*, 240), becoming, through the imagistic language alone, the surrogate of the twin serpents, who had just fled to Athene's temple "with their gliding/slithering" (*lapsu*, 225). The associations of serpents and fire is far more extensive and richer than this sample can suggest. The real serpents here, agents of deception working through fire, will eventually become the real flames of Troy's destruction.

Night falls suddenly, hiding in its darkness the deception of the Greeks (250–2), as sleep comes for wretched men, the most welcome gift of the gods (*mortalibus aegris*, 268, a Homeric formula); but it "comes" with a telling suggestion, *serpit* (269, at line end). Now, for the first time in the narrative, Aeneas introduces himself: he is sleeping at home, and he will have us follow him to the very center of his city and back again. He will be more of a spectator than a participant in this second section of his story, as he finds his way through the confused tumult to Priam's palace. He will then direct our view from the palace doors, through to the innermost courtyard as if it were the axial porticoed garden of a Roman house, to the central altar, where the king – the religious and civic representative of Troy – will be sacrificed by a new sort of hero. Here is the very center of the book and the death of the city itself.

The fall of Troy is a continual presence throughout the *Iliad*, the inevitable climax of the ten years of siege. Everyone in antiquity knew Hector's words to Andromache, "There will come a day when sacred Ilios will perish, and Priam, and the people of Priam of the ash spear" (*Il.* 6.448–9), and to recall Hector's words Virgil needed to say only, "The final day, the inescapable moment has come for Troy" (*venit summa dies et ineluctabile tempus / Dardaniae*, 324–5). One would expect the epic poet to pull out all the stops here, giving us the full tragedy of this event with all solemnity and grandeur. The capture of a city had become a rhetorical set piece for historians and poets, of which we have many examples. The last, futile stand by the brave defenders, the forced entry of the invaders, the weeping and wailing of the captured – all this is the stuff of high drama. We know that Virgil referred to Ennius' description of the fall of Alba Longa; since we don't have the Ennian passage, we can't know how or to what extent Virgil used it, but we do have Livius' brief but highly stylized account of Alba's destruction, which must also be based on Ennius. It appears that Virgil has suppressed the traditional elements of drama and pathos and focused instead on a very different sort of heroism.

Where is the epic grandeur in Hector's appearance to Aeneas? Virgil indicates immediately that this is not the heroic defender of the city, not the best (by far) of the Trojans, not the triumphant hero "who returned with the armor of Achilles, who hurled Phrygian fire upon the Greek ships" (275–6). The Hector who appears in Aeneas' dream is so changed that Aeneas hardly recognizes him. Here is Troy in defeat, but there is nothing ennobling or heroic in this defeat: black with the dust, his feet pierced with the thongs by which he had been dragged, hair and beard matted with blood, with all the wounds he had ever received. Surely these details are purposeful: in the *Iliad* Hector's body was divinely protected from mutilation and decay. Aeneas does not know what to make of this apparition, and in his dream does not seem to know that Hector is actually dead. He addresses Hector as if he were still Troy's hope and salvation ('*O lux Dardaniae, spes o fidissima Teucrum*', 281) and asks why he is so long in coming, where he is coming from, and what is the cause of the wounds (282–6). If Aeneas seems so oblivious of the reality before him, surely we are asked to pay particular attention to it. Aeneas sees Hector only for what he was, Troy's surest (*fidissima*) defense and glory, and is incapable of crediting the reality of the wounds and mutilation that he himself must have witnessed.

Aeneas' disbelief, too, is rather human: at this point of exhaustion and utter weariness of war (283–5) he needs the help and reassurance of a friend and a renewal of faith in the ideal of heroism. He will get neither from Hector, though; he will get only what he will receive from so many others in similar times of need and what he will receive from Creusa at the end of the book: no comfort, no real help, but a simple command, "Get on with it." Hector has no time for useless questions (*vana*, 287) but says simply, "Troy's time has come: take its sacred gods, sail, and found a new city" (289–95). Hector represents a past that is a grim and bloody reality, not the splendid ideal of Homeric heroism, and what he offers Aeneas is not human sympathy but the first intimation of the Roman mission that Aeneas receives.

There is no epic grandeur in the death of Priam either. Here, at the center of both the city and the book, is an inversion of the order of the heroic world. An old man, properly the source of the city's wisdom and guidance, resumes the armor of youth. And just as Laocoon, the priest of Neptune, who had previously been engaged in sacrifice on the citadel (201–2), became himself the sacrificial victim (through the simile of 223–4), so Priam becomes an unholy sacrifice at Troy's altar (*ingens ara*, 513, where *ingens* clearly does not suggest size, but carries the Virgilian etymology "native"). Furthermore, the inversion of heroic values is powerfully presented through the figure of Achilles' son Pyrrhus, also known as Neoptolemus, the "new warrior," who murders Priam's son Poplites before his father's eyes, an inversion (as Priam himself states here, 540–3) of Achilles' respect for what is right and just, when he honored the king with safe passage and returned Hector's body for burial. Throughout this passage (506–58), too, the imagery of fire intensifies again, to be heard even in the name Pyrrhus (in Greek "reddish, fiery"), and to be connected once more with the fire of Laocoon's serpents (e.g., 210–11), the earlier slayers of priest and sons.

The sacrificial slaughter of Troy's religious and civic head (presented as a literal decapitation at 557–8) is an act of barbarism, of a new heroism of inverted values. But it is a reality that Aeneas himself witnessed and is similar to the horror of Hector's appearance. The ideals of the old heroism of Homer's heroes, at least as they professed them, have been turned upside down at Troy's fall.

Other Images of the Destruction of Troy
(6.494–547, 1.450–93)

There are other passages in which Virgil stresses the blind, senseless brutality of Troy's last night. As we take note of them, we should keep in mind two things. First, these scenes are clearly related: Virgil worked on each of his three poems as a whole, and these passages did not take shape in isolation from one another. Second, the vivid brutality that is so marked did not just happen while Virgil's attention was elsewhere. Homer's realism – the realism, for instance, that makes the actual deaths of Patroclus or Hector so unheroic – does not descend to the sustained brutality that Virgil has made so prominent in these scenes. In the traditional set pieces of other poets and historians of the fall of a city, there are the tears and cries of human sufferers, there are tragedy and pathos, but all in measured doses, stylized and kept within the strict limits of convention – that is, they give us heroic defeat and suffering. Virgil gives us the senseless violence of the "new warrior."

In the Underworld, as Aeneas is hurried through the insistent passing of the night to the meeting with his father and Rome's future, he encounters three principal figures from his past – Palinurus, Dido, and Deiphobus. Each has a special significance, made clear by Virgil through associations elsewhere in the poem. Both Palinurus (as we will see later) and Deiphobus recall Troy, and Deiphobus specifically Troy's last night, when Odysseus and Menelaus had mutilated and killed him in revenge for his sleeping with Helen after Paris' death. The figure Aeneas sees is even more brutally savaged than Hector had appeared: "And here he saw the son of Priam, his whole body butchered, Deiphobus, his face cruelly disfigured, face and both hands too, both ears ripped from his head, his nostrils ignobly slit" (6.494–7). Aeneas reacts much as he had to Hector – disbelief and stunned incomprehension: what is this shameful mutilation, he asks, as Deiphobus tries to hide the marks of his "dreadful punishment"? Aeneas had heard (*fama*, 502) only of a heroic death, of Deiphobus finally dying over a heap of the slaughtered enemy, and had given him a hero's burial and an empty tomb on the shore (505–7) befitting "a great warrior descended from the old line of Teucer" (as Aeneas first addresses him, 500).

The reality, as his mutilation shows, was different. It began in the deception of the joy and sleep of that last night (513–14, 522, "a sleep sweet and deep, and very like the peace of death"), and with Helen's treachery, both to the city and to Deiphobus. His story is a replay of the much longer account that Aeneas gave at Carthage: the false joy (*falsa inter gaudia*, 513), the treachery and deception, the same unheroic savagery. Who is Deiphobus? It is certainly relevant that he was "the dearest of Hector's brothers" (*Il.* 22.233–4), for Hector's mutilation is very much with us as we read these lines, and it may be relevant that Deiphobus played a part in the final deception of Hector as he ran from Achilles, when Athene took on his appearance (*Il.* 22.224–305).

There is another set of images of the Trojan war, where we might least expect them. When Aeneas and the faithful Achates enter Carthage in Book I, they make their way, enveloped in a protective cloud, to the temple of Juno at the center of the city. There they see a series of wall paintings showing scenes they know well – Priam's city and the battles fought around it. Aeneas' first reaction is relief: such awareness of their past struggles and misfortunes will assure their safety now (*'Solve metus; feret haec aliquam tibi fama salutem'*, 1.463). "Here is Priam, look," Aeneas says. "Even here heroic glory has its rewards, here there are tears for human suffering, and our very mortality arouses pity" (*'en Priamus. sunt hic etiam sua praemia laudi, / sunt lacrimae rerum et mentem mortalia tangunt'*, 461–2). Much has been made of these lines, perfect, elusive, and so easily isolated from their context. As Aeneas looks at the representation of Priam, his immediate reaction is that even in a foreign land the code of traditional heroism is recognized. *Laus* (plural *laudes*, literally "praise") is the proper term for the posthumous glory that will be the lasting monument (*praemia*) of the hero. In just these few words Virgil evokes the entirety of heroic values. What follows, though, is a disjunction, conveyed by the idiomatic repetition of the verb *sunt* without a connective: "There are rewards for heroism here, *but* there is also pity for human suffering." The recognition of mortality (*mortalia*) is Homer's contribution, his understanding of the essential futility of death: we think of Patroclus, Sarpedon, and Hector. The "tears for the human condition" (*lacrimae rerum*) are purely Virgilian, arising from the recognition of mortality; they are shed elsewhere in the poem and are very different from the tears of Homer's heroes.

Though Aeneas is at first reassured, as he further contemplates this "senseless representation" (*animum pictura pascit inani*, 464) he groans and his tears become uncontrollable (*multa gemens, largoque umectat flumine vultum*, 465). Just how are these scenes "senseless, empty, pointless" (*inani*)? And why does Aeneas' relief turn immediately to anguish and tears, as he looks more closely? What he sees are paradigms of war: "for he saw how, fighting around Troy . . . " (*namque videbat uti bellantes Pergama circum*, 466). *Namque* ("for") needs some attention. First, it gives the reason for what has just been said – here, the reason for Aeneas' anguish. Second, it serves in Latin quite specifically to introduce an *exemplum*, a paradigmatic illustration. The scenes we are about to see are no random snapshots, not simply highlights of the war, but representative distillations of human conduct.

The first scene (466–8) is of the general ebb and flow of battle – Greeks, Trojans, and finally the helmeted Achilles in his chariot. He alone stands out from the tide of battle, and he will be seen several more times on this wall, the greatest hero of the war; but if we expect to see the exemplar of Homeric heroism, we will be disabused. The next scene (469–73) is one of carnage, the slaughter of Rhesus and his men murdered by Diomedes in their sleep during their first night at Troy. They had been "betrayed in sleep," and Aeneas reacts with new tears (*lacrimans*), remembering perhaps the betrayal in the sleep of Troy's last night and the resulting bloody slaughter. This is not a representation of heroic combat, nor is the next scene (474–8), showing "the unequal combat" of Achilles and the "unfortunate boy" (*infelix puer*) Troilus, who had thrown down his arms in flight and, tangled in the reins, was dragged by his own team through the dust. He is the first of many such types we will see in the second half of Virgil's epic – a youth out of place in the real world of warriors, pathetic rather than heroic in a grim death at the hands of a much superior force (here Achilles). Then (479–82) Aeneas sees the solemn procession of Trojan women bearing in supplication a new peplos for Athene, figures of grief and suffering (*tristes et tunsae pectora palmis*); but the goddess turns away, their pain and prayers denied. This is the cold reality of war and of the gods in war. And then (483–7) Achilles yet again, ransoming the body of Hector, which he had dragged three times around the walls. "Ransoming," though, is not what Virgil says, but rather "sold for gold" (*auro vendebat*). Again we see Aeneas' reaction, a huge groan from deep within (*tum vero ingentem gemitum dat pectore ab imo*), as he sees the body of his friend, and Priam too, stretching out his unarmed hands (*manus inermis*) to Achilles. This is not the Achilles that Priam will remember at his death at the altar (2.535–50), as he accuses Achilles' son Neoptolemus of being "degenerate" (*degenerem*, 2.549). The Achilles of these representative images of war is very much the father of Neoptolemus, ruthless, savage, and coldly venal: there is no suggestion here of the compassion that Homer's Achilles finally felt for a father. Aeneas then (488–9) sees himself among other fighters in a lost cause (Memnon in particular), and finally Penthesilea, "a maiden daring to do battle with men," a figure anticipating Camilla, like Troilus out of place, seduced unhappily by the attraction of wealth and glory ("gold" again, 492), deceived at last and ignobly slain.

This is what Aeneas sees, then, at his weakest and most vulnerable moment in the poem, here on the wall of the temple of the goddess whose hatred and anger have brought him to this point, in the center of Carthage, Rome's greatest enemy. Here is the reality of war, as it is for the weakest and most vulnerable, the youth and the maiden, the aged parent, the women in supplication and those who trust in the deceptiveness of sleep. Virgil has clearly excluded any suggestion of heroic glory from these pictures, but instead shows us the exemplary hero Achilles as a figure of sheer brutality, a mercenary thug. These are all scenes, too, of Troy in defeat, and as such are of a piece with the figures of Hector in Book II and his brother Deiphobus in Book VI; and through language and image, as well as in the figure of the degenerate Neoptolemus, they are of a piece with the inversion of the heroic that Aeneas *sees*, again a spectator and a reporter rather than a participant, at the center of Troy itself in the darkness and deception of that last night.

"There are tears for the human condition and pity for our mortality." We now understand why Virgil shows Aeneas repeatedly in tears as he reviews these images, why his initial feeling of relief on seeing Priam and his city had so quickly turned to anguish as he understood the content of each scene. His words to Achates should not be taken out of their context. Here again is the reality, the truth, of Troy, in war and in defeat. Each of these scenes will be replayed again and again in the Iliadic half of the *Aeneid*. The Achilles we see here at Carthage was not invented by Virgil, but is one of the heroes of Catullus' epyllion (poem 64), a new figure in the epic world, of savagery and brutality, of whom we will see more later.

Andromache's Troy Restored (3.294–505)

Troy fallen can imply Troy restored. "If I had my own way, if I could lead my own life as I pleased, not having to do what I must, I would now be rebuilding Troy and caring for what's left of my dear people, and Priam's city would remain, and I would have restored it with my own hands for my conquered people" (4.340–4). So Aeneas tells Dido, as he tries to make sense of his past, future, and unenviable present. Throughout the poem, until the very end, Virgil allows not only Aeneas but the reader as well to assume that Aeneas' mission is the restoration of Troy in a new land, and the whole of Book III is devoted to the quest for Ausonia – some strange land, at least, with some earlier connection with the Trojan people, so vague and remote that at first it could be assumed even to be Crete. And at the center of Book III, in fact, Aeneas comes upon a Troy already restored.

Aeneas' band has spent the winter at the site of Actium, where, to give thanks for their escape from the Greeks, they "celebrated the Actian shore with Trojan games" and set up a trophy of victory (3.278–88). After this pregnant intersection of past and future, spring comes and they sail north along the coast of Epirus to the town of Buthrotum, where an "incredible report" (*incredibilis fama*, 294) comes to them: Helenus, a Trojan seer, is now married to Andromache and rules over a new Troy which they have founded nearby. Astounded, Aeneas "sets out from the port, leaving his fleet on the shore" (*progredior portu classis et litora linquens*, 300). The mission, the purposeful progress toward Italy, is suspended while Aeneas revisits a version, or a vision, of his past.

This excursion not only occupies the center of the book, but is by far the most extensive episode recounted, just over 200 lines (294–505). It falls into three sections: the first encounter with Andromache (300–55), Helenus' prophecy (356–471), and the departure, with Andromache's final words (472–505) – or, as will be clear, a triptych of Past: Immediate future: Past. We will be concerned here only with the outer panels.

Virgil needs only a few sure strokes to establish what sort of city Helenus has built. It is a perfect replica in miniature, a model reproducing every important detail of the old city. As Aeneas approaches, Andromache happens to be pouring a libation at Hector's tomb outside the walls, "before the city in a grove at the water of a false Simois" (*falsi Simoentis ad undam*, 302), and the tomb itself, of course, is but a cenotaph (*inanem*, 304). Aeneas sees the familiar landmarks: "Proceeding, I recognize a small Troy, a pretend Pergama with the appearance of the great one, the dry stream bed of what is called the 'Xanthus,' and I embrace the threshold of the Scaean Gate" (*procedo et parvam Troiam simulataque magnis / Pergama et arentem Xanthi cognomine rivum / agnosco, Scaeaeque amplector limina portae*, 349–51). Later he refers to this "effigy" (*effigiem*, 497) of the Xanthus. The details are telling. I would not think that Virgil expects us to remember that it is spring and that any real Mediterranean river will be in flood, but I do think that his "dry" Xanthus, this effigy, together with this "false" Simois, should bring to our minds the real stream at its most unforgettable moment, enraged and in flood, choked with corpses, in combat with Achilles and his fire.

There is no reality at all in this Troy, this monument to a dead past, lovingly reconstructed by Andromache. No minor character in the whole poem (with the possible exception of Creusa, so closely related) is drawn with more depth, precision, and feeling than is Andromache. She lives only for Hector's memory, and Hector, yet again, is Troy. As she stands at Hector's empty tomb, she sees Aeneas and Trojan arms approaching, and, terrified at the sight of something supernatural (*magnis exterrita monstris*, 307), she faints. Her whole reality has become something unreal, and her life is lived with and through death. She is no longer capable of grasping what is real and alive. When she recovers, she says, "Are you a *true* appearance, a *true* messenger – are you *living*? And, if this is *death*, where is my Hector?" ('*verane te facies, verus mihi nuntius adfers, / nate dea? vivisne? aut, si lux alma recessit, / Hector ubi est?*', 310–12). Aeneas answers, "Yes, I am alive . . . Be assured, what you see is real, true" ('*vivo equidem . . . ne dubita, nam vera vides*', 315–16).

For Andromache, only what is dead and gone is intensely real, her only reality. She lives entirely for the past and in the past, in a world of shadows and sadness. She has suffered extraordinary personal loss and has survived, but she lives on only with her memories and in this miniature replica of past greatness, a grand lady, left alone in a small apartment among her mementos and photographs in silver frames, consumed by three concerns – her infant son Astyanax, murdered when Troy fell, and Hector, and the heroism that was his and Troy's and that is no longer.

When she has recovered from fright and disbelief, she tells Aeneas of her servitude to Neoptolemus (who again is the new reality of war) and of her marriage to Helenus, "a slave to a slave" (329, again the reality of the present). Then she asks Aeneas of his lot, but specifically of Ascanius: "What of young Ascanius? Did he survive, is he still alive? whom to you with Troy – " (*quem tibi iam Troia –*, 340, perhaps the most expressive half-line in the poem). She cannot complete either the phrase "with Troy *destroyed*" or the thought, overcome by the reality of her own loss, and, when she begins again, she thinks of mother and son: "But even so, does the boy have any love for his lost – mother?" ('*equa tamen puero est amissae cura parentis?*', 341). And then she thinks of Hector and heroism, of the old ideal, not the reality: "Do his father Aeneas" (she does not say "you," as if she were still not able to recognize the reality before her) "and his uncle Hector arouse in him the old heroism and heroic bravery?" ('*antiquam virtutem animosque virilis*', 342), and with that she weeps.

She and Aeneas will have the last exchange at his departure. Heroic gifts had already been offered by Helenus to Aeneas (gold, ivory, silver, and the armor – pointedly – of Neoptolemus, 463–9) and to Anchises (horses and allies, 469–71), when Andromache brings out her own gifts, robes embroidered with gold and, for Ascanius, a Phrygian cloak (482–5). She addresses not Aeneas but Ascanius, saying, "Take these gifts, my child, to remind you of me and to recall the abiding love of Andromache, Hector's wife" ('*accipe et haec, manuum tibi quae monumenta mearum / sint, puer, et longum Andromachae testentur amorem / coniugis Hectoreae*', 486–8). She is again Hector's wife, just as Aeneas had called her at their first meeting (319). "Take these final gifts of your people, you who are the only image remaining to me of my Astyanax, for thus he was, his very eyes, and hands, and face; and now he would be a young man too, just the same age as you" ('*cape dona extrema tuorum, / o mihi sola mei super Astyanactis imago. / sic oculos, sic ille manus, sic ora ferebat; / et nunc aequali tecum pubesceret aevo*', 488–91). "Image" is too weak a word: "ghost" may be too vivid, but it conveys the force of Virgil's *imago*. Yet again we see the sadness of a life lived out among the ghosts of a transfigured past, to the extent that what is present is unreal and even the boy whose face she sees and whose hands she holds is but another ghost; we can hear again her first words of disbelief – "Are you true? do you live?"

Both times Andromache speaks, she thinks of Creusa. The *Aeneid* presents us repeatedly with close human relationships severed again and again by war and the demands of heroism. We experience here the pathos of loss involving mother and child. This is another instance where we can see Virgil at work, reflecting on the larger significance of these representations of mother and child, composing separated passages as one, and thereby going far beyond the pathetic. The final image of fallen Troy at the very end of the previous book was of Creusa, an image literally (*imago*, 2.773, 793), and one that we will recall in other contexts. Except for two brief moments, her words to Aeneas are impersonal and formal; she has come only to announce the mission, the journey to Hesperia ordained by "the will of the gods" (*numine divum*, 777) and by Jupiter himself. She speaks of "long exile and a vast sea to be plowed" (*vastum maris aequor arandum*, 780), an image of futility that Aeneas will repeat verbatim in his answer to Andromache's parting words ("You have rest: for you there is no sea to be plowed," *nullum maris aequor arandum*, 3.495). The future she announces so coldly is to include a new wife – "prosperity and a royal wife; don't cry for your beloved Creusa" (2.783–4). So she had begun, denying him his human grief: "Why do you want so much to indulge this mad grief, my dear husband?" (*'quid tantum insano iuvat indulgere dolori, / o dulcis coniunx?'*, 776–7). As so often, Aeneas' mission has no place for human emotion, for tears and sorrow.

These first words are not entirely Creusa's, though, or Virgil's, but rather Homer's and Hector's, when Hector speaks to Andromache for the last time, just as Creusa to Aeneas here. Hector, removing his great helmet, has just taken Astyanax into his arms and prayed that his son will be a greater warrior than his father, "that having slain his enemy, he will bring back the bloody spoils, and his mother will rejoice in her heart" (*Il.* 6.480–1). Hector then returns the child to his wife, and, seeing her tears, speaks his final words to her, "Dear one (*daimonie*), do not grieve for me overmuch in your heart" (486). *Daimonie* may have been a term of endearment, but Virgil heard it with its commoner, etymological sense, "possessed by a spirit, mad," and transferred it in Creusa's speech as an epithet to "grief" (*insano dolori*). Here is Virgil's allusive artfulness: by this one touch he has made sure that we appreciate how specific is his allusion to Homer's scene.

One final detail must be added. Creusa's ghost announces the beginning of the mission that will, generations later, lead on to Rome. Here, with Aeneas' enforced departure from Troy, is his future and the Roman epic. There are to be no tears for "your beloved Creusa," no indulgence in "insane grief." But Creusa cannot help herself, in spite of Jupiter's commands and divine will. "O my beloved husband" (*'o dulcis coniunx'*) escapes from her lips at the very beginning, and again, in her last words, she thinks of her son with human emotion, "and now farewell, and keep the love of our common son" (*'iamque vale et nati serva communis amorem'*, 789). Creusa has become the impersonal voice of Jupiter and the Roman future, but, through the appeal Virgil makes to Hector's farewell to his wife and child, she still thinks, and causes us to think, first and last of the human loss she too has suffered.

Returning our attention now to Andromache's restored Troy near Buthrotum, we can see it clearly for what it is. Andromache has been allowed to go home again, after extraordinary suffering, but her new city is a pitiful restoration of what Troy had been, and her life is a death among the images and ghosts of her past. Aeneas, who has turned aside briefly from his journey to visit her, must go on, still thinking that he will yet establish another Troy of his own at the Tiber, a kindred city. We have seen the brutal reality of war and Troy's final night, and we have now come to a vivid and moving understanding of what it means to live among the ghosts of the past: even at this early point in the epic we can have little confidence in any new Troy that Aeneas will someday found.

The Trojan Games (5.104–544)

Books I, III, and V are all books of the sea. In a literal sense they are books of wandering and of search; their common element is insubstantial and not to be trusted; and in each a storm occurs which drives the Trojans from their main mission (the quest for Italy) and forces them upon a significant detour. At the beginning of Book V Aeneas is driven to revisit another manifestation of his Trojan past.

The opening lines of the book show us Aeneas already far out at sea, resolved and certain, holding his course toward Italy, but looking back to the walls of Carthage bright with flames. The elements are significant: Books II and IV are land books, and their dominant element is fire. When the ships are out of sight of land, with nothing but sea and sky around them (5.8–9), a sudden storm arises with the darkness of night. "I would not hope to reach Italy in this weather," says the helmsman Palinurus to Aeneas (17–25). "The winds are against us. We must yield to Fortune and turn wherever she calls. We are not far from Eryx, if only I remember correctly and can retrace our course by the stars." Aeneas can only agree: "Change the course" (*'flecte viam velis'*, 28).

This storm hasn't just blown up by chance, nor is it the work of Juno, as was the storm in Book I, nor does it arise simply because the reader might welcome a bit of excitement at sea. Its purpose is thematic – to drive Aeneas from his determined course to Italy and back to Troy and his father. Aeneas takes the occasion of this unexpected return to Sicily to establish an annual celebration in memory of his father with funeral games, the climax of which will be the *ludi Troiani*, an elaborate equestrian performance by the youth led by Iulus, and restaged in Virgil's time by Augustus. This will be our final extended visit to Troy before landing in Italy, and our last major detour to the past.

Of all the twelve books of the *Aeneid*, Book V has the least general appeal. It had the misfortune to have been set between IV and VI, which any book would have found a hard lot in life, but, worse still, what does it offer but a tedious account of some rather derivative athletic contests and a final scene of ship burning? None of this seems particularly entertaining or gets Aeneas any further along. Why should we care? If we can sit through these games yet again, perhaps an answer to this question will emerge. In many ways Book V is as rich as those that precede and follow it.

Virgil begins with the finality of death. These are funeral games, in honor of the dead parent, whose genius, in the form of a snake, receives the offering at the tomb (84–93). Aeneas offers a four-line prayer to his father (80–3), in which we hear echoes of Catullus' funeral poem to his dead brother (poem 101) that intensify Aeneas' realization of the absolute finality of death. It was not permitted (*non licuit*) for Anchises to reach Italy, nor for Aeneas "to seek with you the Ausonian Tiber, whatever it is." The futility of any attempt to reclaim the dead is tangible in the simple adverb *nequiquam* ("in vain") that Aeneas shares with Catullus. This emotional prayer is to be remembered in all that follows: the games, as an offering to "the paternal shades" (*umbraeque paternae*, 81) will be equally futile, and this celebration of the Trojan past will be no more substantial than Andromache's restored city. The games will be different in one respect, though: they will anticipate the city to come.

There are to be four contests – a boat race, a foot race, boxing, and archery. Overall, there is an observable pattern and purpose. First, each event begins with a stylized evocation of the heroic, with specific recall of events and heroes of Troy; and the very fact that Virgil's games are derived from those given by Achilles in honor of Patroclus in *Iliad* XXIII immediately takes us to the fields of Troy. Second, athletic contests were in origin, and to a large extent still are, military exercises and training in which combat has become ritual and bloodless spectacle: no one is killed. Finally, if these games begin as rituals of war, they eventually become almost surreal – not just the harmless games of warriors at play, but disturbing inversions of the reality of war.

It is to be expected that each contest is viewed at first through the magnifying lens of high epic. The ship captains are effulgent in purple and gold, their crews crowned with poplar wreathes, bodies gleaming with oil (132–5). The runners pour forth from the starting line "like a storm cloud," and Nisus opens a gap "swifter than the winds or winged thunderbolts" (317–19). The contestants are motivated by the ideal of traditional heroism, as the boxer Entellus, who excuses his initial reluctance to come forth on the grounds of his advanced years – "it is not that my love of heroic renown has lessened, nor has my (desire for) glory, beaten down by fear" (*non laudis amor nec gloria cessit / pulsa metu*, 394–5); and later (454–5) he is aroused by anger (*ira*), shame (*pudor*), and an awareness of heroic valor (*conscia virtus*), so that his blows fall as fast and thick as hail stones on a roof (458–60). The spectators, too, create an aura of heroic spectacle, as (for instance) when the woods, shores, and hills resound to their cheers as the boat race begins (148–50, where the stylized tricolon adds greatly to the effect). And just as Achilles had "set up the mast of a dark-prowed ship" with a dove bound to it for the archery contest (*Il.* 23.852–5), so does Aeneas, all by himself, somewhat incongruously perhaps; but Virgil seized the occasion to adopt a Homeric formula to underscore this mighty deed: adopting the Homeric phrase *cheiri pacheiei* ("with a thick/mighty hand"), he has Aeneas raise the mast with "his huge hand" (*ingenti manu*, 487). The phrase, and perhaps the task itself, seemed to Servius so incongruous that he took *manu* in another sense, "*magna multitudine*," that is, "with a large band of men."

One of the runners is Diores, son of Priam (*regius egregia Priami de stirpe Diores*, 297). Entellus' huge boxing wraps, which once belonged to Eryx, are made of the hides of seven huge oxen (400–5) – again so incongruous as to be slightly comic if it were not for the obvious reference to Ajax' famous seven-layered shield (*Il.* 7.222–3). His Trojan opponent Dares "alone used to contend with Paris" (370) – another allusion to Troy that calls attention to itself in that the Paris of the *Iliad* would make a very unlikely boxer; and Dares, too, had defeated, at Hector's tomb, a certain Butes, "huge of body," the son of the infamous boxer-king Amycus (371–4). An equally odd Trojan connection is effected by the unusual apostrophe to Pandarus (the brother of the archer Eurytion), "O most famous, you who once, when ordered to confound the treaty, first shot your arrow into the midst of the Achaeans" (495–7), foolishly persuaded by Athene to wound Menelaus (*Il.* 4.73–147) – hardly a heroic deed. And lest we miss this connection, Eurytion then invokes his brother Pandarus as he takes aim (514).

There is something rather unsettling, then, in Virgil's preparation for these games – a tension that arises from a certain distortion in his creation of the epic setting, similar to that in Aeneas' hyper-epic killing of the seven deer in Book I, and a tension that increases in this collection of unexpected, and often distinctly odd, Trojan and Homeric associations. Here again we should realize that Virgil has purposefully selected these associations, just as he did in his scenes of the Trojan war on the temple at Carthage: if strange details are to be found in this poem, they were put there intentionally.

We may add one more example of an oddity worth attention, perhaps the oddest of all these Trojan associations. There are four ships in the boat race, each named for a monster – Pristis, Chimaera, Centaurus, and Scylla. Three of their captains are the ancestors of later Roman families – Mnestheus of the Memmi, Sergestus of the Sergii, and Cloanthus of the

Cluentii. Only Gyas, the captain of the Chimaera, is not given the distinction of a Roman connection. Virgil's description of Gyas' Chimaera, too, is decidedly odd. It would seem to be an aircraft carrier, racing against destroyers, because it is "huge with a huge mass, the work of a city," with three banks of oars manned by Dardanian youth (*ingentemque Gyas* [sci. *agit*] *ingenti mole Chimaeram, / urbis opus, triplici pubes quam Dardana versu / impellunt, terno consurgunt ordine remi*, 118–20). Would this ship really have been so huge, or (as we have seen elsewhere) is this repeated epithet (*ingentem . . . ingenti*) used in the particular Virgilian sense of "native," suggesting that something of the "inborn character" (*ingenium*) is important about this ship? And what is the meaning of *urbis opus* – in what sense is this ship "the work of a city"? And, given the Roman connections of the other boats, is it significant that this one is singled out as being manned by *Dardanian* rowers? Is it significant that the Chimaera gets three whole lines here, whereas the other three get only one and a half or two lines each? Do all these details mean something, and, if they do, why does everything seem to point to Troy? I have no answers. We will have to watch Gyas and his ship particularly closely as the race develops.

This, then, is the first stage of the overall pattern we are observing – Virgil's insistence on the Homeric and Trojan associations of the contests. Our second stage follows from this. As we noted, games are nothing other than training exercises or ritual combat, where there is no death at the end.

In the boat race, for example, Sergestus finally begins to pull away from Mnestheus at the turn (both trailing, in third and fourth places), until Mnestheus makes a spirited and encouraging exhortation to his crew ("Comrades of Hector, whom I chose at Troy's fall," 190 – another reminder of Troy): "I don't need to win (let those be the winners, as you, Neptune, decide), but it would be shaming to finish last" (194–7). Noble and pious words, indeed, and rewarded when Sergestus runs his ship up on the rocks that are the turning point. The final struggle is grandly heroic (227–31), as Mnestheus pulls even with Cloanthus in the final stretch and perhaps might even have overtaken him, had not Cloanthus in turn offered a prayer and vow to the gods of the sea, which was heard and rewarded with enthusiastic unanimity by a whole retinue of the sea nymphs of Phorcus, by Panopea, and by Portunus himself (233–42). Such divine concordance is rare in Homeric combat, and a hero's prayer for victory is rarely completely granted, but in this contest, success attends upon noble piety.

So, too, in the running race, at the end of which everyone, even the unlucky Nisus and Salius (who had clearly been cheated of a sure victory), receives a prize, as at a children's birthday party. And in the boxing match, when Entellus slips and falls, he is raised by Acestes ("pitying him," *miserans*, 452) and goes on to win. Those who fall in actual combat are killed, and bad luck (the *fortuna inimica* that befell Nisus, for instance, 356) means death. Mnestheus claims not to care about victory (*non iam prima peto Mnestheus nec vincere certo*, 194), but in battle there is no second place, no consolation prizes, no pity for the loser.

The boxer Entellus is not only saved by Acestes, but returns to the fight like a man possessed, until Aeneas puts an end to his savage fury (*iras, saevire*, 461–2) and spares Dares. This is all play, where savagery can easily be halted. Entellus then, with one blow, sacrifices the bull that is his prize, "a better life in place of Dares' death," as he pointedly says (483–4). Nisus and Euryalus are the first to come forth for the foot race, and Virgil's readers know what real war will mean for them. After them comes Diores, distinguished as the royal son of Priam. We will not meet him again until his death in the final book, when he and his brother Amycus are killed by Turnus – not simply killed, but decapitated and their bloody heads hung from his chariot (*curruque abscissa duorum / suspendit capita et rorantia sanguine portat*, 12.511–12). This is what it means to lose in war.

We have arrived now at the third stage of our observable pattern and purpose – the aura of surrealism that hangs over these games. They begin (the first stage) with all the drums, trumpets, and banners of heroic confrontation, as when the boat crews, awaiting the starting signal, feel an idealized thrill of anticipation of battle: "Their hearts beat fast and loud in fearful high emotion, and an intensified thirst for glory leaves them weak" (*exsultantiaque haurit / corda pavor pulsans laudumque arrecta cupido*, 137–8). But these are simply games (the second stage), with no blood or slaughter, with prizes for all, where losing, or finishing second, or sometimes even winning, seem hardly to matter. The reality of war has been turned upside down. But Virgil's inversion can at times go beyond the creation of what is unreal, can do more than simply make war into play. Suddenly, watching these games, we are struck with the absurdity of it all, with an unnerving sense of loss of all direction – the surrealism of our third stage.

Returning again to the boat race, we feel this unease as we watch Gyas and the Chimaera at the turn. This was the ship, huge and "the work of a city," that seemed to be distinguished from the others as particularly Trojan – though by suggestions only, with nothing explicit. The Chimaera takes an early lead (no lumbering battleship this, after all), and Gyas, "first and victorious" (*princeps . . . victor*, 160) urges his helmsman Menoetes, an older man (*iam senior*, 179) of experience and caution, to hug the turning mark closely. But the helmsman, fearing the submerged rocks (*caeca . . . / saxa timens*, 164–5), goes too wide, allowing Cloanthus in the Scylla to turn just inside. "A huge agony blazes forth" in the young man

Gyas (*tum vero exarsit iuveni dolor ossibus ingens*, 172), who, with tears and "forgetting all seemly propriety and the safety of his crew," seizes Menoetes and flings him overboard (173–5).

We must try ourselves to exercise some caution here, lest we turn too closely rounding the Rocks of Allegory. Can't we just feel satisfied with a vividly dramatic incident at a crucial turning point in an exciting event? Virgil gives us, in a wonderful miniature, the reckless fire of competitive youth confronting the experienced caution of an aged helmsman. Certainly, even if this ship is strangely Trojan, we ought not to listen to that voice that whispers "Priam," nor should we allow ourselves to take notice of that passing mental shadow that adumbrates the cautious and retiring Latinus, leaving events to the impulsive fire of the young Turnus. Virgil is no allegorist. But the scene isn't quite finished.

> But when, finally and barely, the aged Menoetes emerged from the depths,
> weighed down, water cascading from his sodden dress,
> he made for the top of the rock and sat down on its dry ridge.
> The Trojans laughed at him as he fell, they laughed at him swimming,
> and they laugh at him now as he vomits up floods of salt from his gut.
>
> (178–82)

What sort of laughter can this be? This is no longer good, clean fun. This is the laughter of mockery and derision, a reaction of almost inhuman cruelty in the face of suffering. We cannot ignore what we have just seen, the experience of age assaulted and humiliated by the angry passion of youth. *Sunt lacrimae rerum et mentem mortalia tangunt* (1.462). So Aeneas to Achates, as he looked at the scenes of indiscriminate and senseless violence portrayed on Juno's temple at Carthage. Invert those scenes of the savage reality of war and turn them into harmless exercises, mere sport, and those tears for the human condition become the mocking laughter of the Trojans here.

We hear this laughter again as Sergestus' ship limps back from this same rock on which it has run aground at the turn. As the others were receiving their prizes, Sergestus has scarcely gotten his Centaurus off the rocks, with the oars on one side shattered, a source of derision, without honor (*inrisam sine honore ratem Sergestus agebat*, 272), like a snake run over in a road (273–80). We hear it again, too, from Aeneas himself, as he looks at Nisus, covered from head to foot with the blood and dung on which he had slipped in the foot race (*risit pater optimus olli*, 358). Through inversion, the tears of the real world have become, in these games, laughter at misfortune and derision of the defeated.

The Transformation of Troy (5.485–544)

Virgil's Troy did not end with its fall. The past, whether of an individual or of a nation, lives on, continually transformed, reinvented, serving different needs. These games that we have been attending, though, as we think back on what we have seen, would appear to mark or celebrate a definite end. As we saw, they are occasioned by an enforced return to Acestes' city, as the storm drives Aeneas from his certain course to Italy, and they celebrate the anniversary of Anchises' death: they are, most certainly, funeral games. As the games proceed, we become aware of a thematic finality as well. Here, in Book V, on the eve of their arrival in Italy after seven years, the Trojans replay their epic past one last time, after which the heroic world of the Trojan past can never – in Virgil's poem, at least – be the same again. Play has stood the world on its head, making combat meaningless without death, making the heroic virtues valueless and human suffering insignificant or irrelevant, turning tears into the laughter of derision. Troy must continue to exist for the Trojans in Italy, yes, but for the reader of Virgil's epic it will no longer be the Troy of Homeric epic, nor any other Troy that had existed in the reader's mind when he read the first line, *arma virumque cano, Troiae qui primus ab oris*. . . .

Troy cannot ever end, but it is clearly transformed at this crucial detour between Asia and Europe, east and west. We have said little about the final game, the archery contest. It begins with the usual epic hyperbole and insistence on Troy, some details of which we noted earlier. The order in which the four contestants will shoot is decided by lot, with Acestes himself to go last. Now the role that king Acestes has been given in this book has been purposefully established by Virgil. His mother was an exiled Trojan and his father a Sicilian river, as we are told at his first appearance (38–9), and his mother seems to have been named, conveniently, Troia (so at 61, *Troia generatus Acestes*); but he has assumed the role of a native Trojan (*Dardanius divinae stirpis Acestes*, 711) and becomes almost a surrogate for Anchises. "Would any land be more pleasing to me," asks Aeneas as he orders Palinurus to head for Sicily, "or where I would rather direct my exhausted ships, than that which keeps Dardanian Acestes for me and holds in its embrace the bones of father Anchises?" (28–31). Acestes is "father" (*pater*, 521) as he shoots, and he is addressed as "father" (533) by Aeneas when he awards him special honors for his shot, an elaborate bowl which Hecuba's father had once given to Anchises, a token of significance (535–8).

The contest itself, while more interesting than Homer's version, is predictably routine. Hippocoon hits the mast and the tethered dove flies up in alarm, Mnestheus then severs the cord, and Eurytion hits the dove, by this time flying high toward the dark clouds. "Father" Acestes, left without any opportunity for the prize, nevertheless demonstrates his skill with a shot into the air.

> Then, for all to see an unexpected portent occurred, to be afterwards
> of great import; only later its full meaning became clear
> and prophets then sang dire omens.
> For the arrow as it flew in the bright clouds caught fire
> and marked its course with flame and, consumed, disappeared
> into the air, just as often shooting stars in flight
> cross the sky and draw out their trails like hair.
>
> (522–8)

The language of these lines has the resonance and mystery of prophecy itself. The import of this supernatural occurrence (*monstrum*) will be revealed only by future prophets; only later will it become clear why this blazing arrow appeared so like a comet trailing its tail.

We met this shooting star before, when Anchises had refused to leave Troy (2.692–700). To review briefly, in July of 44 BC, following the funeral (or "victory") games celebrated by the young Octavian for Julius Caesar, a most opportune comet appeared – clearly the soul of the deified Caesar, clearly recognizing as well the piety of his adopted son who had given the games. This "Julian star" (*sidus Iulium*) soon became a fixture on coins and seals. It was placed by Octavian over the statue of Caesar in the Forum and was represented on the pediment of the planned temple of the new god (not completed until 29 BC), which itself, with its altar in front, marked the spot where his body had been cremated. The comet became iconographically as important as the representation of *pietas* to be seen in Aeneas' flight from Troy.

Ancient poets did not care to draw a distinction between shooting stars (meteors) and comets. Both were stars that had become "detached" (*refixa . . . sidera*, 527–8), blazed through the night sky, leaving a trail behind (*crinem . . . ducunt*, 528), and were ominous. The entire sequence of the games in Book V (some 500 lines) thus reaches its finality in this one shot by Acestes, acknowledged by Aeneas as nothing less than the will of Jupiter, for which Acestes receives as a prize the bowl that establishes a traditional connection with father Anchises and Troy. The funeral games, given by Aeneas for his father, "for whom it was not permitted to reach Italy" (82–3), have been, at a stroke, transformed into the games given by Octavian for Julius in July of 44 BC. The Trojan past, having reached a finality through the unreality of Virgilian inversion, has suddenly, with this dread omen, become the Roman future.

The *lusus Troiae* (5.545–603)

The contests are over, but there is one exhibition to follow.

There had existed at Rome for some considerable time a tradition of an equestrian ceremony, a stylized cavalry performance by young men, known as "the games of Troy," *lusus Troiae*. Some modern scholars have supposed that the "Troia" in question had nothing to do with Priam's city, but is only an antiquarian restoration, an attempt to make sense of an unintelligible word originally having something to do with ritual movement or perhaps a labyrinth; but in any case the ceremony was very old indeed, and for the Romans Troy was Troy. We know only that the performance was revived by Sulla, probably for nationalistic and self-promoting purposes, then later by Julius, and then by Agrippa in 40 and 33 (as we happen to be told), presumably as a part of Octavian's developing program: Virgil's account (5.545–603) assured its continuation as a regular event under Augustus.

Here is the final ceremony of the games for Anchises, celebrated in his name but honoring Troy as well, funeral games that began with the recognition of the futility of contact with the dead, with the past. At the same time, in this final performance by the youth of Troy, we look ahead to the Roman future of the Julian *gens*, who, in this particular and in other matters, were attempting to establish their own contacts with the Trojan past.

No sooner has that significant prize been awarded to Acestes than Aeneas sends a certain Epytides with instructions for Ascanius (548–51): let him lead out his young troop (*puerile agmen*) in honor of his grandfather. As in the case of the names of the ship captains in the first contest, the names of the leaders of the three companies here are all of historical significance (563–72). The first company is led by Priam, named for his grandfather; he is the son of Polites, the same one murdered by Neoptolemus at the altar as Priam watched; his "splendid line will swell the number of the Italians." The second is led by Atys, "from whom the Latin Atii are descended" (568), and no one needed a "Peerage" to know that Octavian's mother (Atia) was a descendent of this *gens*. Iulus himself led the third, "handsome in appearance before all others" (570). The line between Troy and the Rome of Octavian could not be more simply and boldly drawn: the transformation of Troy has been completed.

In this celebration of past and future, however, in all this pageantry of the parade field with its drums and trumpets and flying banners, Virgil has inserted some disturbing details, just as he had in the previous games. Again, the result is to leave us with some uncertainty, with a feeling – and no more than a feeling – that the pageantry we see is indeed a "game of Troy" (*ludo*, 593), that all is unreal (*pugnae . . . simulacra sub armis*, 585) and at any moment can become even surreal.

For a moment, the ghost of Dido is to be seen, unmistakably. Iulus rides a Sidonian horse given him by Dido "to be a remembrance of herself and a pledge of her love" (*quem candida Dido / esse sui dederat monimentum et pignus amoris*, 571–2). Virgil's phrasing strikes like a heavy hammer: just some 35 lines previously the prize awarded Acestes was, we remember, a bowl given to Anchises by Hecuba's father, "as a remembrance of himself and a pledge of his love" (*sui dederat monimenta et pignus amoris*, 538). What is Dido doing here, with such a poetically forceful presence? Certainly this is not Rome's great enemy. On the contrary, she becomes for a moment as much a part of Aeneas' past as his father Anchises and his Trojan home – both Acestes and Dido are associated with tokens that are "a remembrance and a pledge of love." Even at this most nationalistic of displays we are made to sense Aeneas' personal loss, the real cost of this empty spectacle. Dido's ghost will be seen again, on similar occasions.

As the three companies weave their intricate patterns, attacking, retreating, and coming together again in peace, their movements are compared to the Cretan labyrinth:

As once the labyrinth on lofty Crete is said
to have had a passage woven of blind walls and the uncertain
perplexity of deception in its thousand ways, where wandering
thwarted any sign of a way out, ungraspable, with no return.

ut quondam Creta fertur Labyrinthus in alta
parietibus textum caecis iter ancipitemque
mille viis habuisse dolum, qua signa sequendi
frangeret indeprensus et inremeabilis error.

(588–91)

Like the wonderful simile in Book VI comparing the Underworld appearance of Dido to a new moon barely glimpsed through a mist, this changes everything. We no longer see the formal patterns of cavalry exercises we were admiring just a moment before, but rather figures lost in a maze, trying desperately to escape, to recover a way out, inextricably wandering, blind and deceived. It is indeed surreal. All of Aeneas' Trojan past, transformed so clearly into the Roman future, all so distinctly represented in this game of Troy to be re-enacted and applauded in its Roman transformation – this entire vision now appears to be the interminable wandering of the blind. It comes to us with yet a further overlay: Virgil, through the language of his simile, makes us experience all the hopelessness of

Catullus, whose world of civil war, of loss and deception, can be summed up in the labyrinth in his epyllion (*ne labyrintheis e flexibus egredientem / tecti frustraretur inobservabilis error*, 64.114–15). Ariadne will extricate the hero Theseus from the Cretan labyrinth only to be deceived and abandoned herself.

Reality finally returns with the burning of the ships, though this itself is an act of madness induced by divine deception. Ascanius is the first to respond to the alarm and the sight of smoke rising from the shore. He confronts the women's madness ('*Quis furor iste novus?*', 670), riding up in haste from the games and revealing his identity by hurling away his helmet (*galeam ante pedes proiecit inanem / qua ludo indutus belli simulacra ciebat*, 673–4). Again, Virgil makes it clear that we have been watching only a sham, the mere appearance of war, represented now by the helmet cast aside, "empty."

This book of the sea closes, as it had begun, with Palinurus, whose name means "the wind that blows back." The storm had driven the Trojans back to Sicily, to the games for father Anchises, and to Troy. At the end of the book, as the fleet nears Italy in the calm of a night voyage, Palinurus is no longer required: the transformation has been effected, the Trojan past has become the Roman future – or at least the *simulacra* of what is to be. Palinurus, though faithful, innocent, and protesting, is overcome by Sleep and flung violently overboard, another victim of deception in the quiet of night. There is to be no return, and thus no need of the Trojan helmsman to guide them: Aeneas takes over the wandering ship (867–8), expressing – though, as always, only to himself – his grief for the loss of yet another friend: "O you who trusted too much in the calm of sky and sea, you will lie now, Palinurus, naked on an unknown shore" ('*o nimium caelo et pelago confise sereno, / nudus in ignota, Palinure, iacebis harena*', 870–1).

Troy has been many things for Virgil and his Roman reader, but for Aeneas ultimately it comes down again and again to the same thing: to deception and the loss of all that had been most dear to him. The story of his past ends here with Palinurus.

5

Rome, the *rerum imago*

If the past in the *Aeneid* is continually distorted by memory and especially by our need to reshape it, then the future must be subject to even greater distortion. For the Greeks and the Romans, the future was unknowable, far more so than it is for us. Over the last century we have come to feel a greater confidence in predicting the future than has ever been felt before. We wake up in the morning to learn what the weather will be for the day, and even for the next three days, with (we must admit) extraordinary accuracy. We have and rely on forecasts of all sorts in our economics and politics, and we have the latest odds and point spreads available from our friends in Las Vegas for most sporting events. We can know of many cancers and other serious physical conditions often before we can feel any symptoms, and we know immediately of epidemics when they have hardly begun. In general, the future becomes ours more certainly with every passing decade.

For the Romans and the Greeks, or for our great-grandfathers on the farm, there was no such feeling of confidence. To read the *Georgics* with real understanding, for instance, we must try to imagine how important weather was to an Italian farmer, how all those signs that predict the weather were a real and necessary body of knowledge, how unreliable they actually were, and how devastating a sudden storm could be, just when the harvest was almost ready. We need to make a constant effort to reconstruct a time when we cannot know, other than by rumors and alarm, that an invading army is a three-days' march away or that a plague has been spreading through the towns and cities just across the mountains to the north. To learn about the future, the Greeks frequently and famously consulted oracles – again something that we must make a real mental effort to take seriously – with two consistent results: the oracular pronouncement was always enigmatic, and misinterpretation was inevitable. It is a curious fact that in both Greek and Latin the words meaning "to look ahead into the future" actually use prefixes meaning "back" (*apo-* in Greek, *re-* in Latin). Jupiter, for example, is angered that Aeneas at Carthage is no longer "looking ahead to the cities given him by fate": *fatisque datas non respicit urbes* (4.225, and so also Mercury, 275: *respicere* is the usual word for looking into the future). One can conclude that, whereas we walk down the road of life looking into the future as we go, the ancients sat in a railroad car facing to the rear, seeing only where they had passed; to see where they were going, they had to look back over their shoulders. This, in fact, is a far more realistic conception of the future than ours.

Many more examples could be given, and much more could be said. What we have just suggested is obvious enough, but we still need to make a constant effort, in this and in so many similar areas, to see the world through the eyes of those at the time. Why, for instance, does Aeneas appear so dense, never getting the message, as he stumbles through Book III? Doesn't he know that he can't stay at Carthage? Why does he need Mercury to bring him the message from Jupiter, and why does he require so many other warnings and so much prompting throughout? If we understood the future as Virgil's readers did, such questions would never be asked.

We have seen what it is to regain Troy, whether to rebuild it as Helenus and Andromache had, or whether to restore it in ritual or in the historical memory of a people, or whether to reshape it in images an individual can live by. Rome is the city of the future, with its own images. We know, of course, that what was the unknowable and therefore deceptive future for Aeneas was for Virgil's readers historical fact: Aeneas did not know what was to come, but they certainly did. But this is where we can easily go wrong, right from the start. First, in this poem there is no such thing as historical fact or any certainty about our past: images and ghosts, deceptions and fantasies are all we have of what has gone by, even a moment ago. Second, this is a poem about Aeneas, and it is his future and the visions he is allowed of the Rome to come with which Virgil is concerned: his readers must approach these visions and see them as Aeneas did. When we read of the Rome to come, we are to see projections that have no more reality than the images of Troy. The Trojan dead and the Romans yet to be born are both shades in the same Underworld.

There are three major previews of Roman history in the *Aeneid*, to which this chapter is devoted. Rome is as ubiquitous as is Troy, taking as many different forms, and we will have many more occasions to observe it. The three major panels, though, obviously call for special and detailed attention on their own. In Book I (254–96) Jupiter tells Venus not to worry, that her Rome and its glorious destiny still stand secure. In Book VI (756–892)

Anchises in the Underworld shows Aeneas the great Romans waiting to take their places in the world above. In Book VIII (626–728) Aeneas receives from Venus the armor made by Vulcan; on the shield appear "the whole line of descent from Ascanius and all the wars fought in order" (628–9). In these three previews all of the greatness and grandeur of Rome is to be seen, its achievements and its divinely sanctioned mission. At the start, let us take note of three important points. First, as the poem progresses and the complex of associations grows more dense, so there is an increasing complexity in these previews. Second, each preview is offered as a consolation or exhortation by a parent to a child upset or distressed: in the narrative these previews have a common purpose, not simply to stage a parade or display of the growth and grandeur of Roman *imperium* before a national audience, but also to calm and encourage and reassure a child faced with an uncertain and overwhelming future. Third, each preview is concluded with dramatic detail that returns us to the narrative in such a way that we suddenly see all that has just been revealed in a very different light.

Jupiter's Revelation (1.254–96)

Jupiter's revelation to Venus in Book I has the simplicity of an outline offered in the first lecture of a course in Roman history:

Aeneas: the war and 3 years of rule (lines 261–6)
    Iulus: 30 years of rule at Lavinium; Alba Longa (267–71)
        Troy and Rome: 300 years of Alban kings, Romulus (272–85)
    Julius: *Troianus Caesar*, the descendent of Iulus (286–8)
Eventual peace: under Augustus, though not named (289–96)

As well as of content, there is a simplicity of chronology here, evident in the numerology (3 + 30 + 300 = 333) and in the economy of detail (only the major players and the main events are cited). Thematically, the Rome to come is closely and repeatedly identified with Troy. Because of Iulus, Alba Longa is prominent and Julius Caesar becomes "Trojan." Peace, unmistakably Augustan, will eventually come at the end of the wars set in motion by Aeneas and necessitating the Martian walls of Rome's beginning.

    (There is one point here that calls for caution and comment. Briefly, and for those with particular interest, many scholars take the *Troianus Caesar* and *Iulius* of lines 286–8 to be Augustus, not Julius, and thus take these lines and those that follow to refer by name to Augustus, with no mention of Julius here at all. It seems to me, though, that the "Trojan" Caesar, who then is specified as the Julius descended from Iulus, "whose rule is bounded by Ocean, whose fame by the stars," would more probably suggest the deified Caesar. *Hunc* ["this one," 289] would be Jupiter's nod or gesture to indicate one who will someday [*olim*, 289] *also* be invoked in prayer [*vocabitur hic quoque votis*, 290]: without the reference to the divine Julius just preceding, the *quoque* here makes no sense. Roman poets are hesitant to refer too openly to the deification that they assume to await Augustus, and always avoid naming him when they do so. Finally, the structural linking of Aeneas and Augustus [*hunc*], Iulus and Julius, seems to me pointed and elegant, and can be paralleled elsewhere – see, for example, Tibullus 2.5, which may depend on Virgil's scheme.)

All is simple, mathematical, neat and clean, and is delivered by Jupiter with a smile of paternal condescension – the same expression with which the father of men and gods calms universal storms (254–5) – and a kiss on the filial cheek. And so he begins: "Spare your fear, the fate of your people remains unmoved for you" (257–8). Jupiter has seen precisely what has so upset his daughter: her fears are all for her city someday to rise on the banks of the Tiber, the Rome that will be a consolation for the loss of Troy (238–9). Glory and power are her sole concern and the sole focus of Jupiter's response. The Homeric backdrop for this scene tells all. Thetis, in the first book of the *Iliad*, hears her son Achilles weeping in distress on the shore; she goes to him as a mother, comforting him with a caress, and asks why he is so unhappy. She then goes to Zeus, who acknowledges human grief and responds to a mother's concern. What we see in the *Aeneid* is very different. If this were the only occasion in the poem on which Venus shows no maternal sympathy for Aeneas' suffering, we might not want to make too much of the contrast with Thetis, but it is characteristic of Venus to be concerned for Aeneas only as the agent of her future city. After her opening words to Jupiter, she never again mentions her son directly. Achilles weeps, and is consoled by a sympathetic mother. The only tears in Virgil's account belong to Venus, and they are not shed for the distress of her son but from her fear that he will be barred from Italy. Venus weeps for the power and glory of her future city, and she, not Aeneas, is the child to be consoled.

Jupiter has spoken in heaven, and our attention is now directed back to earth. "Thus he spoke, and sent Mercury from heaven to assure that Carthage receive the Trojans with hospitality, that Dido, in ignorance of what must be, not bar them from her land" (*ne fati nescia Dido / finibus arceret*, 297–300). Dido's ignorance of fate seems to make no sense, and has called for comment and explanation since antiquity. Surely, if Dido knew what was fated to happen – both her own unhappy end and the eventual destruction of her city by Rome – she would do everything in her power to keep the Trojans from her land. But Virgil means exactly what he has said, if we will put aside our preconceptions of what we think he ought to mean. The "fate" in question is certainly Rome's power and glory, all that Venus is fearful about and all that we have just heard from Jupiter. Mercury's mission is to deceive, to perpetuate human ignorance, in order to further the Roman mission. Dido's ignorance of destiny – of her own destiny and her city's – has been divinely assured (*volente deo*, 303), and the god's gift to Dido of inner peace and human kindness (*in primis regina quietum / accipit in Teucros animum mentemque benignam*, 303–4) en- sures from the beginning her own madness and death. Can this be viewed as anything but divine cruelty? Could Virgil have devised a more unex- pected or harsher way of concluding this first preview of Roman history than this juxtaposition of Roman destiny and the individual to be sacri- ficed to it? We will see that Aeneas too receives the revelations of the Rome to come with this same human ignorance, subject to the same consequent deception.

Anchises' Review (6.756–892)

In Book VI Aeneas descends to the Underworld to meet with his father and to learn of his progeny, the famous Romans to come. Both purposes (the personal and the epic) are significant.

"Come now," says Anchises (6.756–9), "I will show you the glory to follow upon our Dardanian offspring, what descendents await from our Italian line." Troy and Rome are one people. The parade has the expected con- tingents – the Alban kings, Romulus as the founder of the city, the Roman kings, and the *clari viri* of the Republic, with special emphasis on Augustus. (The review proper ends at line 853, with the well-known lines on the Roman imperial mission: the passage on the two Marcelli is an addendum – *addit*, 854).

The historical record presented here, though, is far more complex than was Jupiter's in Book I. Strict chronology has not been observed. We can see two halves:

760–807: The Alban kings (760–76)
           Romulus and the glory of Rome (777–87)
           [!Augustus (788–807)]

808–853: The Roman kings (808–16)
           The Republic (817–53), but interrupted by
           [!Julius Caesar and Pompey (826–35)]

Augustus and Julius/Pompey have not taken their proper positions in the line of march and thereby call particular attention to themselves. Augustus not only follows immediately after Romulus and his city and is granted by far the largest space in the parade (17 lines), but after him the splendor and glory of the whole procession often seem rather questionable. There is thus a distinct difference between the two halves: we view the heroes of the first half with confidence and pride, but, after Augustus has gone by, the famous men who follow often raise some doubts about their qualifications and accomplishments. The division, then, is not primarily chronological, but depends rather on the clarity of our perception of those who pass: the Alban kings, and Romulus himself, belong to fiction and romance, but with the Roman kings real history begins, and real men parade before us. If this is what Virgil intended us to see, then his inclusion of Augustus as the grand marshal of the first group is very significant.

What splendid men are these Alban kings (to whom the same amount of space is devoted, 17 lines, as to Augustus)! "What young men! What strength they display – look!" says Anchises (771–2), "with the civic crown shadowing their brows." They all wear the *civica corona*, the garland of oak leaves awarded to Augustus in 27 BC as an honor in perpetuity, in which he took special pride. But their glory belongs to a past so distant that the names associated with their great deeds have been all but forgotten – so we can take the suggestion of the line that closes their passage, if we read it as a contemporary of Virgil ("these [towns that they will build] then will be known, but now they are lands without names," *haec tum nomina erunt, nunc sunt sine nomine terrae*, 776). The mists of a distant time, we can say, seem to have obscured any reality.

Romulus passes next, distinguished as the son of Mars (*Mavortius*) and Ilia, the descendent therefore of Assaracus, one of the legendary founding fathers of Troy (777–9). There is no mention of his brother Remus – no suggestion of the fratricide is allowed to cloud this foundation. Romulus is all divine glory, but most of our attention is directed to the Rome of the seven hills, of imperial power and Olympian splendor, not the village of huts on the Palatine.

"Now turn your gaze here, to this people and your Romans. Here is Caesar and all the line from Iulus to come under the vault of heaven" (788–90). Again there are scholars who take this Caesar to be Augustus, but again the pairing with Iulus makes it, in my view, much more likely that this is Julius. But Augustus follows immediately, *Augustus Caesar, divi genus*, who will bring back the golden age of Saturn to Latium (791–4). Any doubts we (as Republican Romans) might have about Julius are suppressed, just as any second thoughts about Romulus as fratricide were quickly brushed aside. It is quite clear that this is a rather fabulous

Augustus, from the first suggestion of the restoration of a golden age of peace, through the poeticized extent of the Roman *imperium* under his rule, to his impersonation of Hercules and Dionysus. Anchises' description of the Augustan achievement is extravagant in the extreme, but it is the extravagance of imagination and fantasy, and as such acceptable.

Only three of the Roman kings have turned out for the parade. Numa, venerable as always, is a figure of simplicity, justice, and religious observation, but, somewhat oddly, a representative as well of imperial power (*missus in imperium magnum*, 812). But the other two kings clearly are figures of a sort we have not seen before. Tullus (Hostilius) will shatter his country's peace and will move the citizens again to war (815–15); much more of his character will be revealed later. Ancus (Marcius) is not a man we can admire: he appears here as a boastful demagogue (*iactantior Ancus / nunc quoque iam nimium gaudens popularibus auris*, 815–6). These are real men, ambitious in arms and with a thirst for personal power. Something has changed.

The Republican heroes are led by Brutus. "Do you wish to see the Tarquin kings and the arrogant spirit . . . ," Anchises begins, and we can easily supply his next words, assuming that it will be Brutus who will take vengeance on their arrogant spirit. But it isn't at all: Anchises completes his sentence, ". . . of the avenger Brutus, and the *fasces* of power that he took over from them?" ('*vis et Tarquinios reges animamque superbam / ultoris Bruti, fascisque videre receptos?*', 817–18). There is no other way we can read these lines: this is a Brutus who continued both the regal power and the arrogance of Tarquinius Superbus, and, lest we be in any doubt, Virgil goes on to equate the new consular power with the "savage axes" of the royal *fasces* (*consulis imperium hic primus saevasque securis / accipiet*, 819–20). Brutus was the Roman paradigm of love of country and of justice, to the extent that he ordered his sons put to death, and watched their execution, for attempting to restore the Tarquins. But for Virgil, Brutus' love of country was compounded with an excessive thirst (*cupido*, "lust") for heroic renown, for glory (*vincet amor patriae laudumque immensa cupido*, 823). Subsequent generations have got it all wrong, according to Virgil: Brutus was driven to execute his sons by the acceptance of and total obedience to his heroic mission, and is to be pitied for it (*infelix, utcumque ferent ea facta minores*, 822). This is one of the great themes of Virgil's new epic: the heroic ideal can never be pure, and the reality will inevitably involve a terrible human cost.

The Decii, Drusi, Torquatus, and Camillus – these stand for the early heroes of the Republic and are disposed of in two lines (824–5). Then (in a panel of 10 lines) Anchises points out Caesar and Pompey, "concordant spirits now and while they are covered in this night below," but what war, what slaughter they will bring about if they reach the light of life. This is not the Caesar we have seen before, paired with Iulus, but the dictator responsible for civil war, appearing with a reality totally different from the pageantry of the first half of this parade; and it is Caesar, not Pompey, at whom Anchises points the finger of blame. "Don't, my children, become so inured to war," cries Anchises (the vocative *pueri* is direct and emotional); "don't turn your armed might against your country's belly. It is yours [Caesar's] to be the first to yield, yours, you who are of divine descent – you, my own blood, throw down your weapons!" (832–5).

Other Republican heroes follow, some who spread Rome's power abroad against Troy's Greek enemies or in the subjection of Carthage, but some, too, who were protagonists in the civil unrest like the Gracchi and Cato. But Virgil's primary focus is clearly on the very beginning and end of the Republic, its inherent character. What Brutus did, "from love of country and vast thirst for heroic renown" gone wrong, is exactly what Julius Caesar would do later – the "savage axes" of the *fasces* in the first instance turned against the consul's own children, and in the second the sword of Anchises' own descendent (*sanguis meus*, 835) turned against his own people. This is what Aeneas has come here to see.

Here are the consolation and exhortation given by a father to his son at a time of doubt and hesitation. Anchises reminds us of this at the very end of the first half of the parade, when he says rather unexpectedly to Aeneas, "And do we still have misgivings about the heroic mission that lies ahead in Italy, or is it fear that prevents your settling there?" (*et dubitamus adhuc virtutem extendere factis, / aut metus Ausonia prohibet consistere terra?*, 806–7). We should pay attention to this aside, realizing that it is very hard for an epic poet to attribute openly and often such fear and doubt to his hero, without creating a Jason. Fear and doubt have brought Aeneas to the world of the dead, a journey granted to a select few. But there can be no human embrace with the dead father he has sought and whom he finally meets – no consolation, then, from this *imago*, once a father. Instead, in return for this supreme act of *pietas* he receives an exhortation, a parade of passing shades, mere pageantry to begin with and then, as Roman *imperium* is clearly visible, the reality of the costs of political and national power gone wrong.

Anchises concludes with those continually stirring lines of the Roman mission: "You, Roman, be mindful of ruling the peoples of the world with your power (this will be your contribution) and of setting a standard for peace, sparing the conquered and humbling the proud" (*'tu regere imperio populos, Romane, memento / (hae tibi erunt artes), pacique imponere morem, / parcere subiectis et debellare superbos'*, 851–3). These are fine words, but to whom are they addressed? Not to his son, certainly. This *imago* is like the *imago* of Creusa that Aeneas returned to burning Troy to search for, but which, when found, he could not grasp: both have become the voice of an impersonal, national destiny. Anchises even seems to have forgotten that he is talking to his son: Aeneas has been displaced by, or at best transformed into, a generic Roman (*tu . . . Romane*).

After Aeneas has been properly fired with "the love of coming fame" (*famae venientis amore*, 889), Anchises accompanies him and the Sibyl to the twin gates of Sleep, still telling of the wars to be fought, of the peoples of Latium and their king Latinus, and all that must still be done (889–92). True shades depart easily through the gate of horn, but Aeneas leaves through the gate of ivory, through which "the shades send false dreams heavenward" (*sed falsa ad caelum mittunt insomnia Manes*, 896). Much has been written about this choice of exit, often by those who don't trust Virgil to mean what he says: surely this must be either a most unfortunate mistake by Aeneas or a miscalculation by Virgil. But if it is anyone's mistake, it is Anchises': it is he who, still speaking of all that must be done to further the Roman mission, actually leads his son and the Sibyl to that very gate and sends them forth (*his ibi tum natum Anchises unaque Sibyllam / prosequitur dictis portaque emittit eburna*, 897–8). Nothing could be clearer: it is Anchises who is responsible for sending forth these false dreams, the whole parade we have just watched.

In Book I, after assuring his daughter that her Roman destiny remained unmoved, Jupiter sends Mercury to begin the deception of Dido, the first and essential step in the historical process. Now, after encouraging his son with the glory of Rome to come, Anchises sends him forth through the gate of deceptions. We are reading a poem largely concerned with the images of past and future, after all – images that, however glorious or reassuring, must of necessity prove to be deceptions. All Aeneas can do is to continue – *ille viam secat ad navis sociosque revisit* (899), by now a familiar refrain.

The Shield of Aeneas (8.626–728)

The third preview of "Italian history and Roman triumphs" (8.626) on the shield forged for Aeneas by Vulcan is more complex still. It is, in fact, a study in complexity.

This is the second shield Vulcan has made for a favored hero. On Achilles' shield made just a few years before he had set the world and all human life (*Il.* 18.478–608). In it, to begin with, he had fashioned earth, sky, sea, sun, moon, constellations, and Ocean, and all around, at the end, again the great river Ocean. Within this universe he represented all human activity, too extensive a panorama even to be summarized here – cities at peace and at war; scenes of farming and of bloody battle; of a dancing floor with young men, girls, and acrobats; of kings and judges; of herdsmen playing innocently on pipes and soon to be slaughtered in a cattle raid; of plowmen at work on the dark earth; and of much else, one vignette after another, the extraordinary variety and richness of life.

Vulcan brought this same sense of the complexity of human experience to his second attempt, although anyone turning from Homer's shield to Virgil's must be struck by the inadequacy of the latter. Vulcan did his best work for Achilles, without a doubt, but only because of the limitations imposed by his second subject. Roman history, even with Actium as its finale, simply doesn't have the expressive and emotional potential of his previous material. We must accept this: the complexity of Vulcan's second try is of a different order.

It is a complexity created expressly from the simplicity of the elements – earth, air, fire, and water. As the Cyclopes of Aetna labor (8.445–53), metals of the earth (bronze, gold, and steel) flow in streams, becoming liquid in the fire of the huge forge (subterranean Aetna itself), receiving blasts of air from the "windy bellows," becoming solid once again as the fiery material is tempered in water. Homer's world of human activity is set within the universe; Virgil creates the Roman experience, characteristically, from the elements themselves.

The Homeric model was important for Virgil in a second respect, which will also help us in our initial disappointment. Anchises had expressed his reactions with no uncertainty – his grief for the young Marcellus, his pride in Augustus, his compassion for, and outrage at, Brutus, his anger with Pompey and Caesar. No similar cues are offered the reader for the scenes on Aeneas' shield, just as Homer offered no judgments or commentary. On Achilles' shield we see what is there to be seen, and so as well on Aeneas' shield: reactions, emotions, and judgment are left entirely to the reader.

Structurally, at least, the passage is simple – "the wars fought in (chronological) order" (629):

I   630–45: Romulus, Remus, and the kings of Rome
II   646–70: the Republic
III   671–728: Augustus and Actium

Though we had been promised "the whole line of descent from Ascanius" (628–9), we see nothing of Alba Longa or its "Julian" kings, and there is a glaring imbalance – some 40 lines devoted to Roman kings and the whole Republic, and nearly 60 to Augustus.

The first panel (the Regal Period, basically) is a triptych: first a scene of pastoral innocence, then of violence and subsequent peace, then of savagery, all seeming to form an intended sequence. First, Romulus and Remus appear together as babes suckled by the she-wolf, who licks them alternately with maternal affection. They are absolutely fearless (*impavidos*, 633) in their innocent acceptance of this beast which so often stands in the European memory as the paragon of animal ferocity, and the scene is set, of all places, in "the verdant grotto of Mars" (*viridi . . . Mavortis in antro*, 630). There is no hint of the fratricidal foundation to come, no *Mavortia moenia* rising, but rather an innocent harmony of babes and wild nature in a pastoral setting attributed to Mars.

Next we see the rape (*sine more*, 635) of the Sabine women, the ensuing battle, and the subsequent peace (635–41): an act of violence, its consequence, and resolution.

The third scene is worth spending some time on. Of all the six kings after Romulus, and of all the great events and deeds that Vulcan could have chosen, we see only Tullus (Hostilius), the exemplar of war who traditionally initiated the ceremonies of war. We had a brief sight of him in the Underworld, as one who would shatter the peace (*otia*) that the country had enjoyed under Numa and drive the citizens again into arms (6.812–15). There are no ceremonies in this scene, no wars that rouse and unify the spirit of a people grown complacent in their leisure. Tullus is engaged in the punishment of the Alban Mettus for his perjury (8.642–5). Not only do we see the body torn apart by the four horses, but there is Tullus himself, "dragging the guts of the traitor through the woods, and the underbrush was wet with the dew of his spattered blood." The historian Livy, Virgil's contemporary, in his account of this event (1.28.10–11), provides a relevant comment: "All turned their eyes from the sight of such brutality. This was the first and last instance, among the Romans, of a punishment so unworthy of the laws of humanity: in other cases we can take pride that no other people have established gentler punishments." Now in Livy's account the destruction of Alba Longa follows immediately, a direct consequence of Mettus' perjury. We need to recall, at this point, how Jupiter had stressed the connection of Alba with Troy, its founder Iulus ("Ilus he had been called, while Ilion still stood," 1.268), and the 300 years of kings "under Hector's line;" and we need to remember as well the pride with which Anchises had pointed out some of the Alban kings (6.760–76), all associated directly with Troy as descendents of Aeneas. How striking it is, then, that we see, of all that Vulcan might have chosen from the period of the Roman kings, this graphic scene of violence, so barbaric and "so unworthy of the laws of humanity." Virgil does not remind us that this was the end of Alba Longa, that Alban perjury was the cause of the city's destruction, nor does he make any connection with Laomedon's perjury that was the ultimate cause of the destruction of Troy (as Dido remembered, 4.542). He offers no overt reminder, either, that Iulus' city was the ancestral home of the Julian family, who were among the Albans relocated to Rome at this time. For Virgil's readers, no reminder was necessary.

From the four elements all things were made; from them Vulcan has created a range of Roman experience that is a counterpart to the variety of human experience represented just before on Achilles' shield. This first panel of Rome's beginnings shows us the full extent of the city's character, from innocence and natural harmony, to violence, war, and peace, to the extreme example of barbarity. Like Homer, and as is appropriate for a work of visual art, Virgil offers no comment: just as was the case with the scenes of the Trojan war on the temple wall at Carthage, we see what is there to see.

There is a similar range of experience in the scenes from the Republic (646–70). We see Horatius at his bridge, and Cloelia, and Manlius holding the citadel – heroes and defenders of the city. But the Gallic enemy is given equal space. They are actually in possession of the citadel and, like the Greeks seizing Troy, "are defended by darkness and the gift of blind night" (658). What is more, they are worked in an anaphora of gold (*aurea ... aurea ... auro*, 659–61), an inspiring sight. Here are priests and devout matrons, but also the punishments of the world below, where Cato gives laws to the pious and Catiline receives his due (666–70). Again, we see the whole range, the variety, of Roman experience, the good and the bad, and all without comment.

We have been looking at the scenes on the periphery of the shield only. Far larger is the single scene at the center – the sea and, upon it, the battle of Actium and its aftermath.

We can no longer avoid the crucial question, though we can provide no answer: what did Virgil really think of Augustus, the new *imperium*, and the Augustan peace? Historians find no agreement about the real man and the realities of his rule; the pendulum swings back and forth, and there can be no certainty. About Virgil's view the possibility of certainty is even smaller. We can only try to arrive at an impression that is consistent with our understanding of the rest of the poem.

Virgil's images of the Trojan past range from the idealizing to the starkly realistic, with, somewhere in between, a blending or blurring of the extremes in images that are strangely surrealistic. In the increasing complexity of these images of the Roman future, we have observed a similar range. Virgil, too, has found a variety of ways to remind us that all our conceptions of past and future are, and must be, nothing other than images, all without reality and all therefore deceptions. Jupiter's words of reassurance to Venus close with a vision of Augustan peace: "Then wars will cease and ages of savagery will turn mild" (*aspera tum positis mitescent saecula bellis*, 1.291), and then the doors of the temple of war will be closed and Madness (*impius Furor*) will rage harmlessly, chained within. When "the rough ages grow mild, with war put aside," we are looking ahead to a new Golden Age, which for Virgil is always an ideal, a hope and a dream, but never a reality. (Line 291 stylistically calls attention to itself, as Catullan: it is a "golden line" with a verb of three long syllables [a molossus] in the middle: for three of these in a row, pointing clearly to Catullus in an idealized Golden Age context, see Virgil's "Messianic" Eclogue, 4.28–30.) Romulus and Remus will return as law-givers, as brothers (1.292–3) – another dream; and Furor, chained, will rage in vain. There are those who can find a reality here – I cannot.

Anchises' glance happened to fall on Augustus just after the idealized Alban kings and after his description of the glorious city at the height of its power, to be founded by Romulus. Augustus was eulogized similarly, without restraint and in idealized terms, as we saw. It is only after he has passed in review that disturbing facts about Rome's character begin to emerge. Again, many readers of the *Aeneid* find Augustus' restoration of Saturn's golden age in Latium (as predicted by Anchises, 6.791–4) nothing other than a statement of fact.

What of Augustus on the shield, then, set within all the scenes of the Roman experience that we have just observed? The battle of Actium is to be seen (*in medio classis aeratas, Actia bella, / cernere erat*, 675–6) set in "the golden image of swelling sea" (*imago aurea*, 671–2). There is Caesar Augustus, leading the Italians into battle "with the Senate and People, with the Penates and the great gods" (*cum patribus populoque, penatibus et magnis dis*, 679). Let us pause here briefly to admire how Virgil connects this culmination with its beginning, as Aeneas sets out from Troy, "with allies and his son, with the Penates and the great gods" (*cum sociis natoque, penatibus et magnis dis*, 3.13). Augustus is "standing on the lofty stern, twin flames leaping joyously from his temples, the Julian star above his head" (*stans celsa in puppi, geminas cui tempora flammas / laeta vomunt patriumque aperitur vertice sidus*, 680–1).

We will see Aeneas later, returning by sea to his besieged camp, "standing on the lofty stern" (*stans celsa in puppi*, 10.261) and holding high, as a sign, this very shield, all aflame. As the Rutilians see him, his head is aflame and the golden boss of his shield belches huge fires (*ardet apex capiti cristisque a vertice flamma / funditur et vastos umbo vomit aureus ignis*, 10.270–1), "not otherwise than when bloody comets glow red in the clear night" as dire omens or the parching heat of Sirius brings disease and death for wretched mortals. Vulcan's helmet belches fire even as Aeneas receives it, turning it over in his hands in wonder (*terribilem cristis galeam flammasque vomentem*, 8.620).

Here is that dense web of Virgilian associations, in which our urge to find the rational answer must stick every time. The Augustus at the center of the shield and the Aeneas who holds it aloft have become one, and both are absorbed in the fire of war that blazes forth. A rational answer can be had perfectly easily. Both are figures of righteous might. Augustus is fighting and will defeat the barbaric forces of the east, the Olympians will overcome the monstrous gods of the Nile, and the triple triumph will be celebrated to mark the victory of Roman *imperium* over the conquered peoples of the world. All this we can see on the shield, just as we heard of the Roman mission from Anchises ("to rule the peoples of the world, to establish a standard for peace, to spare the conquered and to crush the proud," 6.851–3), and just as Jupiter proclaimed. After this battle, reason might tell us, the golden age of Saturn will be restored (we have Anchises' word for it, 6.792–5), and, with the end of all war, the savage ages will grow gentle (as Jupiter assures us, 1.291–6).

Poetic sense, though, is at odds with such a rational answer. There is no more reason to feel confident about the reality of a restoration of peace and a new golden age here in the *Aeneid* than there was in Eclogue 4. These visions of a coming time of peace belong to the future twice over: they are in the poem's narrative future, Aeneas' future; and they belong to the future of Virgil's reader as well. The poetic reality is fire, by means of which the arms of Vulcan were forged, the element that unites Aeneas and Augustus through the shield. To believe in the return of universal peace or in the stability of peace, we must imagine a world without fire.

As Venus delivers the armor to her son, she seeks to dispel the same doubt that Anchises had reassured him about: "Here is the finished work of craft, the gifts promised by my husband. Do not doubt after this to seek the proud Laurentians in battle, or fierce Turnus" (613–14), and with these words she seeks his embrace (*dixit, et amplexus nati Cytherea petivit*, 615). This, and the brief hand-clasp in Book II (592), are the only times in the poem that there is any contact at all between this mother and son, made particularly notable in the light of the other occasions when Aeneas has tried to embrace those near to him. There is nothing maternal in this embrace, however, as her words make clear: she is delivering the arms terrible in their fire (*terribilem cristis galeam flammasque vomentem*, 620) and that will ensure her own victory.

After Aeneas has looked upon the *non enarrabile textum* ("complexity beyond description," 625) of the shield, however, and Virgil resumes his narrative, it is a different matter: "He marvels at all this on the shield of Vulcan, the gift of his parent, and rejoices, all unknowing, in the image of history, lifting on his shoulder the story and fate of his offspring" (*Talia per clipeum Volcani, dona parentis / miratur rerumque ignarus imagine gaudet*

/ *attollens umero famamque et fata nepotum,* 729–31). Here again is human ignorance, recalling Dido kept by divine intervention in ignorance of Rome's history (*fati nescia,* 1.299). Here too are the false dreams that Aeneas, guided by the shade of his father, took with him as he left the Underworld through the gate of ivory, the "image" of Roman history to come.

6

Virgil, His Life and Works

The *Aeneid* was the work of the last 10 years of Virgil's life, but it did not come from nothing. If we want to know it better, we must consider the times that Virgil lived through and the poetry he had written previously.

His Life and Times

Publius Vergilius Maro was born on March 15, 70 BC, near Mantua and died on September 21, 19 BC, at Naples, where he was buried, on his return from a trip to Greece. (His *nomen* in Latin was spelled *Ve-*, but during his lifetime and continuing through the Middle Ages various connections were made and stories grew up around words like *virga* ["a magician's wand"] and *virgo/virgineus* ["maiden/maidenly"]; the spelling "Virgil" is so rich in tradition that it is a shame to sacrifice it to a bland propriety.) He wrote the *Eclogues*, *Georgics*, and *Aeneid*. So much, though without the dates, we are told in what antiquity believed was the epitaph written by the poet himself: *Mantua me genuit, Calabri rapuere, tenet nunc/Parthenope: cecini pascua, rura, duces*: "Mantua bore me, Calabria took me from life, Naples now holds me. I sang of pastures, fields, and leaders." This is as good a place as any to start, whenever we begin to think of the details of Virgil's life, for the epitaph, though not Virgil's own composition, gives us just about all the facts we can be sure of. Not much was known of Rome's greatest poet when he died, and there were those who were ready to satisfy the ancient appetite for literary biography, the principal form of criticism in antiquity. Details were manufactured from the poems themselves and were collected by Suetonius in the second century in his *Lives of the Poets*, which was used and amplified by Donatus in his *Life of Virgil*. Other poems, too, were attributed to Virgil as youthful works, to be found today under the title *Appendix Vergiliana,* none of which did he write, but it is always exciting to discover lost works of a famous poet, especially if they are early efforts of a genius in the making. What follows here, then, will be more concerned with his times than with his life, since what really matters is what his experience was at the different stages of his life, particularly as he was composing each of his three poems.

Virgil's life coincided with the dissolution of the Roman Republic, the civil wars, and the restoration (for so it was intended to appear) of the Republic by Augustus. Had Virgil lived and written at the end of the previous century, or in the first years of the succeeding, there would have been much less to say. Poetic genius is certainly both shaped and given stature by the historical environment: what might Alexander Pope have written if he had begun to write at the defeat of the Spanish Armada, for instance, or what sort of plays would Sophocles have produced if he had been a contemporary of Menander? The experience of these years at Rome demanded understanding, as such times always do, and the material for a poetic understanding was at hand.

Gn. Pompeio Magno M. Licinio Crasso consulibus ("in the consulship of Pompey and Crassus"): this is how the Romans would have referred to the year of Virgil's birth, in a way far more telling than a numerical date. The year 70 BC marked a definite turning point in the violent and protracted death of the Republic. Both consuls had begun their careers as lieutenants of Sulla, the conservative opponent of the new man Marius, and both knew full well that political power would henceforth belong not to the Senate or the People of Rome, but to the military commanders ready and willing to use their armies. Rome had outgrown its system of government. By 146 it had defeated Carthage for the third time and effectively controlled Greece. Further conquest and the continued spread of influence and control in the Mediterranean had brought vast wealth to the state and to individuals, had transformed the old agricultural economy and produced problems beyond anyone's power to deal with, had made the constitution of Republican government essentially obsolete, and had begun to destroy the entire social fabric. The symptoms of disease had been clear for a long time. The Gracchi brothers squarely faced the problems of the dispossessed farmers, discovered the potential of the tribunate and the People's voting assembly as a means to oppose the Senate and the entrenched families of the aristocracy, and had been murdered. Expansion, the Social Wars, and slave rebellions cast a bright light on other problems but produced only Marius, in solitary opposition to the Senate. Sulla responded with murder and the restoration of the Senate's power. Together they showed what a strong man with an army, loyal to him or bought, could do.

By the time Virgil would have assumed his *toga virilis* after a quiet boyhood in the countryside of Mantua, all the pieces were in place at Rome, poised for the endgame. The secret alliance of 60 BC, later known as the First Triumvirate, had established the uneasy partnership of Pompey, Crassus, and Caesar, working together only to be able to outmaneuver the *optimates* (the controlling aristocratic families) of the Senate, and in 55 the agreement was renewed. Catullus died in this year or the next, leaving a bleak sketch of youthful hope betrayed. Worse was to come. The triumvirate came apart with the deaths of Julia (Caesar's daughter, happily married to Pompey) in 54 and of Crassus in Syria in 53. Total anarchy ruled at Rome, due to the street-fighting of rival political gangs led by Clodius and Milo, to the extent that by the end of 53 no consular elections had been held and the Senate house had been burned down (an apt metaphor for the times) as the funeral pyre of Clodius, the brother of Catullus' "Lesbia."

Virgil was 21, then, when Caesar crossed the Rubicon and anarchy became civil war. We do not know where he had spent these formative years, or where or how he was educated: the ancient biographical tradition conjectured, not unreasonably, that he had studied at Cremona, Milan, and Rome, and eventually (less plausibly) with the Epicurean Siro at Naples, and it was even supposed that his forensic career ended, due to his constitutional shyness, with his first public speech – a little bit of drama obviously invented to explain the fact that there was no public career. What matters far more, though, is to realize that the experience of his first maturity was of anarchy and civil war. On the Ides of March, 44 BC, he was 26 years old, as the second stage of conflict began.

In November of 43 the heirs of Caesar were officially recognized as the Second Triumvirate. Antony, Octavian, and Lepidus were in control of Rome and Italy but at odds with each other, not unlike the earlier gang of three. But there was one great difference: they revived Sulla's proscriptions. Estimates vary, but a reasonable guess of the number of those outlawed is 300 senators – that is, about half the Senate – and 2,000 knights. Not all those proscribed were murdered – even their most famous victim, Cicero, would have escaped had he not turned back back to Rome in his flight to Greece. Some of the proscribed were, like Cicero, political enemies, but what the triumvirs needed most of all was the ready cash that confiscated estates would realize.

In September of 42 BC the Republican armies were defeated by Antony and Octavian at Philippi. Virgil, by this time, was engaged with the *Eclogues*, a book of 10 pastoral poems published in 37 BC or, as now seems more likely, in 35, when he would have been 35 years old. Philippi had resolved nothing, as it turned out. When Caesar had viewed the field of

Roman dead (some 6,000) after the defeat of Pompey at Pharsalus six years earlier, he said, in dismay and resignation, "This is what they wanted" (*hoc voluerunt*). We can wonder whether Antony or Octavian felt anything at all. The Republic had, in effect, disappeared, leaving only the Caesarian faction, and it soon became evident that this was split into an east and a west, with another world war inevitable. In 40 BC open conflict was barely averted when a pact was negotiated at Brundisium; Antony's interests were represented by Asinius Pollio (Virgil's patron, to whom the Fourth Eclogue is dedicated) and Octavian's by Maecenas (whose charmed circle would soon include Virgil). The strained relations continued. In 37 as another crisis loomed, Virgil himself (with Horace, Tucca, and Varius) was part of Maecenas' entourage that made the journey to Tarentum, where the Triumvirate was renewed, though hostilities between the two sides were again barely avoided. Such was Virgil's experience and personal involvement during the period of the *Eclogues*.

We must make a constant effort to think of real time. It is too easy to leap ahead to the next major event on the time line, the naval battle at Actium in September of 31. But from 37 until then, Rome lived through six years, each one of them tense with the realization that another civil conflict was inevitable. In 35 Pompey's son Sextus was defeated in Sicily by Octavian's admiral Agrippa, and with him the unlucky Lepidus was removed from the scene. But even after the final showdown at Actium, Rome remained in a state of tense uncertainty. It was another two years before Octavian and his armies returned to Italy, a period of waiting for the triumphal entry of the same man whose proscriptions 13 years earlier had been so devastating and bloody. As Tacitus acutely summarized the process much later at the beginning of his *Annals* (1.2), even to the Julian faction there was now left only one leader. Octavian paused for a bit near Naples late in the summer of 29 before entering Rome to celebrate his triple triumph, and Virgil read to him the product of these years of unrest and uncertainty, the *Georgics*. A conscious effort of another sort must be made: we must be careful not to look back at this extraordinary moment from the vantage point of even a few years later. The *Georgics* was neither conceived nor completed in a world at peace. Some small progress had perhaps been made. During the composition of the *Eclogues* peace and settled order were barely to be imagined; the *Georgics* took shape over the six long years during which Rome could expect only the worst, and achieved their final form after another two years when the hope of stability and peace was merely a possibility.

It would be a mistake to think that Virgil, when he finished the *Georgics*, only then began casting about for something else to write. All his works form an unbroken continuity, and the *Georgics* leads directly into the

Aeneid, which must have been taking shape in his mind well before 29. Its roots, then, have spread through the same soil that nourished the *Georgics*, though its seasons of growth and maturity were different. These were the years of Octavian's rather tentative steps toward a solution to the problem that Julius had hardly been able even to formulate: how could one man hold monarchical power while the forms of the old Republic could be made to appear restored? It was done slowly, with the constitutional settlements of 27 and 23. Few Romans at the time could have been taken in (Tacitus certainly wasn't, a century and a half later), and we can hardly suppose that Virgil was. The epic was complete except for a few minor details when Virgil died in 19, but the process of shaping Augustan Rome had hardly begun. Again, we must not read the *Aeneid* from the perspective of the Ara Pacis or Augustus' Forum. The hope of peace might shine a bit brighter than it had in 29, but the reality of Virgil's experience, the reality of a lifetime, could hardly have faded.

One of the remarkable things about Virgil's poetry is how constant and unchanging it remained over the years. His concerns were the same when he began to write as they were at the end, not because he remained static, but because the most basic and honest questions we can ask are essentially the same, and allow no answers. The idea of the *Georgics* was forming in his mind as he was shaping (not just completing) the *Eclogues*, and likewise, as we read certain passages of the *Georgics*, we can see shapes and images forming that are the essence of the *Aeneid*, so that it really is possible to have a discussion about the influences of the *Aeneid* on the *Georgics*.

Similarly, each of his three poems is an extraordinarily unified whole, in which themes and ideas recur continuously throughout, shifting, merging, and reflected again and again in different patterns as contexts change. Virgil's manner of work was never linear. He continually rewrote, expanded, and altered what he had already written as he worked on new passages, and these passages could be far apart. For example, the "half-lines" are scattered pretty much evenly throughout the *Aeneid*, from which we can conclude that no book was more finished than any other at the time of his death. As another example, we can tell that certain Eclogues were written before others, and yet the numerical patterns and balances in the Book of 10 poems could only have been achieved by rewriting the earlier poems; and it should be apparent, in any case, that these 10 poems form a unified whole. The great constant in all his poetry was his attempt to comprehend and give shape to the chaos of his time, to find order in the disorder around him. Each of his poems is in itself a reflection of this compulsion to devise order.

The *Eclogues*

None of Virgil's three poems was predictable. After the fact, they each seem so natural, almost inevitable, because his precedent immediately became compelling and continued right up to the present. Pastoral poetry, though, had been only a minor cove in the coastline of Hellenistic poetry, inhabited only by Theocritus, and he only as a summer resident. Then why would anyone think of composing a didactic poem on farming? Hesiod was the obvious precedent, but very little of his *Works and Days* is actually to be seen in the *Georgics*. And the very idea of an epic, "on kings and battles," was anathema at the time to any Roman poet with a pretension to taste and learning. But because each of the three poems now seems so natural, the question "why?" is almost never asked.

What was there in Theocritus' *Idylls* that so appealed to the young Virgil? It was, I think, simply the idea of the power of song to transform reality. The singer can change the world around him into whatever he wants, and that change can be seen, tangible and fully realized, in the landscape in which he sings, and which in fact he has created.

Our idea of pastoral is of shepherds and shepherdesses disporting themselves in a green shade far from the gritty realities of the city. This landscape is ever warm and sunny, the sheep (no cows, please) fleecy and decorative, the simple rustics piping on oaten reeds (whatever they may be) their songs of love (but not too much love). Country versus city, charming simplicity versus modern complexities. This is not where pastoral began, and this is not at all what Theocritus or Virgil intended.

I am confident, though it can hardly be demonstrated, that Theocritus had known real shepherds and herdsmen. He was born in Syracuse in Sicily around 300 BC, a near contemporary of Callimachus, and later lived in Cos and Alexandria. As a boy he had grown up hearing and speaking the Doric Greek of Sicily, which was the dialect too of Cos. He uses this dialect vigorously and unexpectedly in some of his bucolic poems – not to add a touch of authenticity, like oregano or rosemary added to a sauce, but as the real language of his shepherds and herdsmen. Some (though not all) of these figures have come straight to his poems from the fields, such as Comatas and Lycon in Idyll 5. In this poem there is a genuine coarseness, in language and matter, that is the antithesis of our general notion of pastoral refinement, of Marie Antoinette playing the milkmaid. On the other hand, the figures who appear in country masks in Idyll 7, going to the harvest festival at a farm on Cos, are real poets, of the city and of the library, urban sophisticates having a day in the country, and many of Theocritus' other pastoral figures are similar. Idylls 5 and 7 give us the two extremes of the inhabitants of his country: at the one end, the real shepherds, with their language and the direct coarseness of every aspect of their lives, and at the other, the real poets and friends, disguised though they are, out for a day in the country. These are real people, such as appear too in the other poems of Theocritus. His pastoral singers, we must suppose, began as real herdsmen, like those of Idyll 5. (Anyone who wants a vivid and compelling entry into the reality of a shepherd's life should read the extraordinary autobiographical memoir *Padre padrone* by Gavino Ledda, who grew up, illiterate, without even primary schooling, shepherding the family flock on Sardinia.)

This is simply to urge (which is all we can do here) that we see in the countryside of Theocritus a basis of reality that our conditioned response does not often allow us to see when we enter the pastoral world. The shepherds Theocritus knew (and that Ledda writes about from his own life as one of them) were barely distinguishable from the animals they lived with, with whose skins they were clothed. It was a brutish existence, lawless and unregulated, sexually unrepressed, more animal than human. Their days were spent in complete isolation, and in fact in avoiding others so as not to mix flocks, and it is completely believable that in Theocritus' day, as is still the case, a simple pipe provided some relief and pleasure.

If, then, we can accept as a starting point that the real shepherds in Sicily or Cos sang and played for amusement and consolation during days and nights deprived of human companionship, and if we can allow ourselves to imagine that Theocritus, though a city boy, might have spent some time throughout his youth as an observant and curious visitor to the real countryside around Syracuse, as Idyll 7 invites us to do, then we can suppose also that he conceived of the shepherds' songs as the perfect paradigm for the power of his poetry to transform his world too. We read in our literary histories that he created pastoral, but we are not told why he might have done so, except in so far as we are sometimes directed to some shadowy precedent in earlier literature, from whence it all, somehow, then sprang. The shepherds' song, that can transform what is base, coarse, and brutish, and provide both consolation and cure, became pastoral poetry.

We have only a moment to spare for Theocritus, but we can learn much by spending it with his Cyclops. Homer's Polyphemus belonged to a pre-civilized stage of human development: a caveman, literally, living in isolation with his sheep, and a monster and a cannibal. As such he was a perfect paradigm for the real shepherds Theocritus knew, more brute than human. But give him the pipe that Homer neglected to provide him with, and imagine him in love (as any Alexandrian poet would instinctively do), and we have the Cyclops of Idyll 6, noting of course that it is not Theocritus who has imagined him so, but two herdsmen, Damoetas and Daphnis, who, in the midday heat of a summer's day, having driven their herds to a spring, sit down to sing. Daphnis first sings of the Cyclops playing on his flute and thus oblivious to the advances of the sea nymph Galatea: "for often in love what is not beautiful appears beautiful, o Polyphemus" (as the song ends, 6.19). Damoetas' song is the Cyclops' response, saying that he was not oblivious at all but simply playing the game a handsome lover should, for he has seen his own reflection in a calm sea and knows how beautiful he is – beard and eye and teeth as gleaming as Parian marble. The power of song to transform beast into beauty is again the theme of Idyll 11, addressed to Theocritus' friend Nicias, a medical man, since "there is no cure for love, Nicias, other than the Muses" (11.1–3). The exemplar of this assertion is, again, the Cyclops, who sings to Galatea his invitation to come live with him and be his love, and all the pleasures they will prove are a complete revision of the herdsman's reality, transformed through song. At the end, song has indeed been the cure for his hopeless love: in his reformed pastoral world it doesn't matter if Galatea won't respond, because he will simply find another.

This, I think, was what Virgil saw in Theocritus' bucolic poetry, that poetry is a means of reinventing and transforming even the harshest realities of our existence. Virgil, though, saw it more clearly and more imaginatively. We have observed that the realities of Virgil's experience were very harsh indeed – political chaos, social disintegration, proscriptions and confiscations, and civil war that in the years 41–35 showed every sign of breaking out anew. Virgil's book is a way, one way at least, of seeing our world: it is not an escape from reality (as the traditional opposition of country and city often implies), but a means by which the real world can be made acceptable, inhabitable. The *Eclogues* contain the songs of singers who have created a landscape of the imagination in which they can live for a brief time.

As a preliminary to the *Eclogues,* or to anything Virgil wrote, we should be aware of structure. Scholars have discovered a remarkable simplicity of arrangement of these 10 poems, apparent from a number of different factors:

There is, first of all, a clear division into halves: 1 and 6 introduce, and 5 and 10 conclude, each half. Further, the book is composed of balancing pairs of poems, as indicated, focusing on the center in a box-within-a-box arrangement. Finally, there is a progression through the whole collection: the first half is very different from the second half; and, reading in order, our final destination is not one we could have imagined when we started. We might see each Eclogue as a separate movement of a 10-movement symphony, each with its own tempo and character, but all together forming a perfectly progressing whole.

There is another aspect of this arrangement worth a moment of our attention: it is based on an extraordinary numerical pattern, an abstract architecture that could hardly have been apparent to readers and could not have been intended to be. A few simple figures (which have been observed and discussed by a number of scholars in the last century) will make the point. The first four poems have a total of 330 lines, and the first four of the second half have 331 (the slight imbalance seems intended). The pair of 2 and 8 have together 181 lines, and so does the pair of 3 and 7; the pair of 4 and 6 have 149, and the pair of 1 and 9 have 150. What this numerical architecture tells us – and this is the important point – is that Virgil composed the collection as an integrated whole. We will note that certain Eclogues are demonstrably "early" and others "late," and certainly each is to be read as a complete poem in itself. But the balanced arrangement of 10 poems, and the extraordinary care taken with the invisible and inaudible numerical structuring, show us Virgil at work on the book as a whole as the idea of a collection took shape, altering and adapting "early" poems in both content and length, composing and shaping "later" poems not so much as self-contained, distinct pieces, but as conclusions to the whole sequence.

It has often been observed that the *Eclogues* is the first poetry book, not simply a collection of similar poems (such as Catullus or Theocritus had published), but intended to be read as a progression and understood as a whole. Not only does it have a beginning and an end, but its parts somehow seem to echo and resound in sympathetic vibrations in the reader's mind with each other. All three of Virgil's poems were composed in this way.

Let us begin our brief survey of the *Eclogues* with two pairs (3 and 7, 2 and 8) and the concluding poem of the first half (5). These poems are all largely inspired by and based on Theocritean originals and frequently recast Theocritean lines. They consist of the songs of shepherds, either solo (2) or paired (5 and 8) or in an exchange of verses (3 and 7). The settings are an idealized pastoral landscape. And they are all in one way or another concerned with, or illustrative of, the power of singing to transform the harsh realities of the shepherd's experience.

Eclogue 3 begins as if it were going to replay the coarse scurrility of Theocritus' Idyll 5. Menalcas and Damoetas meet and exchange somewhat sanitized insults for some 35 lines, but as soon as they become singers (that is, as the actual contest begins), they are transformed, almost totally. Each puts up a wager, which turns out to be not the appropriate heifer or lamb, but pairs of beechwood cups crafted by a certain Alcimedon, one pair with representations of the Alexandrian astronomer Conon and the Alexandrian astronomical poet Aratus, the other with their semi-divine predecessor and exemplar Orpheus – poet, scientist, and magician (3.36–46). Finally (half-way through the Eclogue, in fact), they begin: not a trace of their old coarseness remains. Damoetas starts the exchange–with the first line of Aratus' poem (3.60). Later they exchange couplets about Virgil's early patron, the politician and poet Asinius Pollio (3.84–7). All of what they sing in the actual contest is similarly very different from those first exchanges *in propriis personis* as shepherds. Eclogue 7, equally Theocritean, is remarkable for the care Virgil devoted to the details of the occasion and the setting. Daphnis, by chance, had seated himself under a rustling oak, and there too Corydon and Thyrsis have driven their flocks (sheep and goats), both young, both Arcadians, both singers (7.1–5). But this is not Virgil, setting up the contest: the "*ego*" telling us all this is one Meliboeus, who, totally in the character of an unsophisticated raconteur, reports with exactitude and in unnecessary and rather fussy detail how he came upon these three (the details occupy all of lines 6–17). The whole poem, then, is the reported reminiscence of Meliboeus (as he reminds us at the end, 69–70), but it is Virgil who has transformed his realistic dithering and fussiness into an Arcadian (that is, imagined) setting, as Daphnis (not Meliboeus) invites us to join him at leisure in the shade, under his poetic oak, amid the buzzing of the bees, at the reedy bank – as it turns out to our surprise – of the Mincius. We are not in Arcadia at all, but just for a moment in Virgil's native countryside. The brief appearance of the Mincius here is like that of Pollio in Eclogue 3, a hesitant trial of what the Virgilian Eclogue will become. There is a wonderful complexity here, beautifully crafted. Pastoral song has created its wonderland, and the Arcadian exchange that follows is no less wonderful.

Eclogues 2 and 8, which form another pair, are equally Theocritean and are clearly concerned with the power of pastoral song. The setting of 2 is important: the rustic Corydon, unhappy in his love for Alexis, whom we find to be a town slave and the pet of his master, used to sing for consolation in the shade of the beech trees (*tantum inter densas, umbrosa cacumina, fagos/adsidue veniebat*, 2.3–4), and now sings this song of his unhappy love alone to the mountains and woods. Corydon's song is that of Theocritus' Cyclops in Idyll 11, and his Alexis is as unattainable as was Galatea. But no matter – love is a disease to be cured by song, and Corydon ends, as had the Cyclops, by assuring himself that he will find some other Alexis. In Eclogue 8 two songs are sung, the first by Damon in the character of a nameless shepherd unhappy in love who ends by threatening suicide, the second by Alphesiboeus in the character of a woman who employs magic to bring back her lover Daphnis. Whether the magic ritual is successful or not, though, is left unclear at the end: "Do we believe? or do those in love imagine dreams for themselves?" (8.108).

The uneasy doubt we are left with at this point is intentional, contrasting as it does with Corydon's facile certainty in the corresponding Eclogue 2. If we view the book as falling into two halves, we can see an intended progression from certainty to doubt and finally to failure. The first half closes (Eclogue 5) with two songs about the death of Daphnis (much like the two songs of Eclogue 8), sung by Menalcas and Mopsus after a thoroughly pastoral introduction (5.1–19). Mopsus first laments Daphnis' death: all of the pastoral landscape mourns for him, but song will ensure his fame forever. Menalcas then sings of Daphnis' apotheosis – song will even bring about immortality. As the two singers at the end exchange gifts, Menalcas gives Mopsus the pipe on which he sang – and he quotes the first line of each – Eclogues 2 and 3.

The remaining five Eclogues are, we can say, Virgilian, and we can suppose that they evolved and took form as a result of Virgil's earlier explorations of Theocritean pastoral. In these poems the setting becomes Italian, and not just by a single incongruent mention of the Mincius. The countryside is not always Theocritus' idealized Sicily or Arcadia, but can be what Virgil himself had known, the small farm rather than the midday grotto with its shaded spring. The real world of Rome and the reality of the confiscations suddenly are now there, with real men (Pollio, Gallus) now among the shepherds. Finally, as the settings become recognizable, the power of pastoral song to alter reality is revealed as no more substantial than the images that it had created.

Eclogues 4 and 6 are another balancing pair, and 6 also opens the second half of the book. Eclogue 4 is best known as the "Messianic" Eclogue, so called because it was seen in the Middle Ages as a prophecy of Christ's coming. Its first line announces something loftier – "Sicilian Muses, let us sing of things somewhat greater" – and what follows revisits Catullus' epyllion, poem 64. Here is something different indeed, and very Roman – a poem for Pollio's consulship (40 BC) that foresees the eventual return to the Golden Age. The poet has left the pastoral setting (the tamarisks and woods, 4.2–3) and the final age of Cumaean song has come. Through the power of this new Roman song the hopelessness and despair of Catullus' present will become an imagined world of peace and sufficiency.

The second half of the book then begins (Eclogue 6) with a similar affirmation of the power of poetry too intricate to go into here; suffice it to point out that the pastoral figure of Silenus, after a ritual binding, is compelled to sing a history of poetry, starting with the divinities Apollo and the Muses, then the semi-divine singers Linus and Orpheus, then Hesiod (elevated by the Alexandrian poets to stand alongside Homer). In the center, though, Silenus sets the poet Gallus, the friend of Virgil, and his reception by the Muses, at which he was given special pipes as a token of succession. The whole Eclogue is a poetic history and an affirmation of revelatory magic.

Eclogues 1 and 9 are clearly companion pieces. Both are very Virgilian: the Theocritean pastoral setting has become Virgil's own, not Arcadian or Sicilian, although not entirely Italian either. The singers in this unreal fusion of landscape are likewise of two worlds. Tityrus is both the singer in the pastoral shade at noon, whose piping has in effect created the imagined perfection in which he reclines, and as well the slave who goes to Rome to get his freedom and land, in the midst of the actual confiscations of 41 BC. Finally in Eclogue 9 we see the power of song for what it really is – effective still to create its own world of the imagination, but in the face of reality having no more power than do "Chaonian doves when the eagle comes" (9.12–13).

Eclogue 1, we must remember, was completed (if not written) last of all, purposely to stand at the head of the collection as well as to complement 9. One shepherd, Tityrus, "meditates" the Muse of pastoral on his slender reed reclining under the spreading beech, while another, Meliboeus, in the confused countryside of the confiscations, his farm seized by a "foreign" soldier, is leaving forever with the pathetic remains of his flock. Tityrus owes his freedom – he speaks of himself as an aged slave – to a young god at Rome, who can hardly be other than the young Octavian (we must remember that this detail may have been formulated as late, possibly, as 35 BC). How are we to understand all this? In antiquity it was taken quite literally and biographically: Virgil himself lost his own farm, but it was restored through Octavian's intercession with his board of three commissioners, Pollio, Varus, and Gallus. Nothing of this is demonstrable historical fact, though persistently repeated by modern critics and historians. On the other hand, we can read what Virgil has written. In Tityrus we have yet another singer whose song has transformed the world around him. But there is a huge difference: elsewhere the reality transformed has been represented, most often, as unhappiness in love, whereas here, at the beginning of Virgil's book, the reality is contemporary, political, Italian, and Roman. Tityrus' freedom, though, as we see it, is no more "real" than his identity as Virgil (he is old, gray, and an ex-slave). What Tityrus represents, though perhaps uneasily and uncertainly, is the final stage in a process of poetic exploration and discovery. Theocritus' pastoral singer, as Virgil's Tityrus, has found himself able to address the events and experiences of Virgil's own time and has been able to transform even the realities of civil war (represented, of course, so aptly by the confiscations of Virgil's Mantuan countryside), as he lies at his ease, piping under his beech. As we begin to read the *Eclogues*, we see nothing less than the supreme vision of what the creative imagination can achieve.

Of course, it can achieve no such thing. Tityrus may remain forever in the shade of his beech, but Meliboeus is driven out. As the shadows lengthen, Tityrus can offer him only the consolation of a single night, "under my leafy shelter, with ripe fruits, chestnuts, and plentiful cheese" (1.80–1): these are the recognizable provisions of Theocritus' singers, the offerings of the Cyclops to Galatea or of Corydon to Alexis. In Eclogue 9, placed near the end of the book, the poetic despair has deepened. Corydon's "dense beeches, our roofed shade" (*inter densas, umbrosa cacumina, fagos*, 2.3, which inevitably recall Tityrus' shady beech) return poignantly in the setting of 9 as "the old beeches, now broken" (*veteres, iam fracta cacumina, fagos*, 9.9), and in this setting pastoral song is no longer possible. Moeris has barely survived, along with Menalcas, and is no longer the singer he was, as he tells Lycidas, his young and still enthusiastic companion on the road to the city. We hear snatches of Menalcas' poetry, as overheard once by Lycidas but now recalled with difficulty – pastoral verses of the old style (9.23–5, 27–9) – but Menalcas himself is absent, and further song must await his coming, as Moeris concludes: "then will be a better time for song, when he himself comes" (*carmina tum melius, cum venerit ipse, canemus*, 9.67).

Cornelius Gallus, Virgil's friend and fellow poet, the inheritor of the pipes of true poetry in Eclogue 6, returns in Eclogue 10. The scene is Arcadia, and Gallus re-enacts the dying Daphnis of Theocritus' Idyll 1. Again, like Eclogue 6, this is a complex poetic weave, which we cannot follow in any detail, but the outline is clear. Gallus, dying of love in these Theocritean surroundings, refuses to be comforted or saved. How could he possibly be? He is, after all, a real man and a Roman general, not a poetic shepherd, as he reminds us. The audacity of Virgil's setting such a well-known figure from the Roman world in this thoroughly artificial Arcadian scene has often been noticed, with some uneasiness, but this was precisely Virgil's intention. The imaginative creations of pastoral song are, at the end, useless. Pastoral poetry began with the premise that the Muses are the only cure for love, as Theocritus had told his physician friend Nicias, and as the Cyclops then demonstrated (Idyll 11). Gallus dismisses this possibility, with some scorn – "as if this were the cure for the madness of love" (*tamquam haec sit nostri medicina furoris*, 10.60). His dismissal is in effect a denial of all that has formed the basic assumption of the pastoral world preceding, that poetry transforms reality – until, that is, the reality of Eclogues 1 and 9. "Love conquers all: let us too yield to Love" are the words of Gallus' final surrender: *omnia vincit Amor: et nos cedamus Amori* (10.69).

The *Georgics*

The *Georgics* is the richest and most perfect work of ancient literature. It is about human nature as a part of the natural world, and yet there is hardly a single human character in it, nor is there any extended discursive analysis of the physical universe. It deals largely with "physics" – that is, our material environment as we perceive it, experience it, and live in it –, and yet it is pure poetry. It is a poem of remarkable simplicity, telling of birth, growth, and death, the essential and inevitable processes of life, and yet so extraordinarily complex are the patterns Virgil created that there is no general agreement today as to what it is all about, and in fact very little has been written about the *Georgics* that even suggests that there is some meaning, graspable and significant, there at all.

Furthermore, it is a poem posing as a handbook of farming that shows real knowledge and some experience of the subject, but from which no one could learn even the simplest agricultural operation.

No one could ever have guessed that Virgil would have begun with Theocritean pastoral as a model. But a poem on farming makes no sense at all. There was Hesiod, whom the Alexandrians set beside Homer as their champion and exemplar, but if Virgil had wanted to become the Roman Hesiod, would not the *Theogony* have seemed a far more likely model than the *Works and Days*? Practical handbooks on farming abounded, in Phoenician, Greek, and Latin, as Varro dutifully recorded in the introduction to his own work on farming, published in 35 BC. Such books were as popular as cookbooks today, but what sort of Muse could possibly inspire a serious poet to versify instructions on plowing or grafting? Why Virgil chose to write on agriculture is a serious question, to which the old answer is patently absurd on several counts – that Virgil, prompted by the powers that then were and the acknowledged instructions of his patron Maecenas, wrote a versified treatise to get the small farmer out of the city rabble and back to his small farm.

The *Georgics* occupied Virgil between the publication of the *Eclogues* (37 or 35) and 29, when the completed poem (as we are told) was read by Virgil to Octavian. The occasion is significant, even if the details, and perhaps the whole story, were invented. After the defeat of Antony and Cleopatra at Actium in September of 31, Octavian had remained for two years in the east and Egypt, securing his victory. Returning to Italy in the summer of 29, he paused at Naples until all was ready for his entry into Rome and the celebration of the triple triumph. The poem he heard during his hours of leisure was about universal forces, at times in creative balance, at times unbalanced, out of control, and destructive. At the most basic level these were the elemental forces of earth, air, fire, and water, always (especially the last two) in opposition to each other. The farmer, with the knowledge accumulated over generations and inherited, can balance these opposing elements to control nature, otherwise wild and unproductive. And yet, inevitably, in spite of all the knowledge painfully acquired and all the artful craft and immense labor with which that knowledge is applied, the oppositions remain – fire against water – and conflict and uncontrollable destruction must result. This was what Octavian, so recently in sole control of the Roman world, listened to, and this was the understanding that Virgil had reached during these years of his life, after so much conflict and destruction appeared to have reached an exhausted cessation.

Since Philippi in 42, the possibility of renewed civil war was always there, as we noted above. The years of the composition of the *Georgics* were hardly a time of peace. In fact, peace was hardly even a hope, as Antony, with Cleopatra's support and the resources of Egypt, gathered forces and established a formidable military power in the east, in readiness for the showdown that finally occurred in September of 31. This was no more a time of peace than the years of our own "Cold War," an interesting name in this regard: tension and fear predominated, with opposing forces balanced against each other and mutual destruction averted by deterrence alone. This is the very stuff of Virgil's great poem.

The movement from the *Eclogues* to the *Georgics* is readily apparent in the landscape of each. The political chaos of Virgil's youth could only be resolved by imposing upon it the Theocritean pastoral setting – Sicilian shepherds, Arcadian song, the piping at midday at the shady pool. Here was peace, or, rather, only here was peace imaginable. Slowly, though, we can see this setting becoming more real, and real figures appear beside those shepherds with Greek names, with glimpses of Varus and Pollio, Varius and Cinna, and with much more than a glimpse of Gallus. The landscape itself changes; the Mincius flows where we would never have expected it, and, though we have no clear map, we are now within walking distance of Mantua, Cremona, and even Rome.

The movement toward reality continues with the *Georgics*: here are real farms, though seldom geographically specific, real crop-lands, orchards, and woodlands. The progression from Arcadia with its idyllic ease (the creation, or fabrication, of the imagined shepherd-poet) to the unrelenting toil of a very real Italian farmer is the progress of a poetic imagination, moving from the world of 42 (in which civil war, proscriptions, and confiscations are the reality) to the world of 31, in which the tensions of an uneasy balance have suddenly found a release, for the moment. Virgil had come much nearer to being able to deal directly with the realities of his world.

The progress from the shaded pool to the field of grain is also that from imagination to intellect. The pastoral poet confronts chaos and unhappiness by the imaginative creation of a setting that excludes the real world: his song transforms reality. This is fine, but it doesn't work, and Gallus, at the end, must yield, as does everything, to human weakness. If the poetic imagination ultimately fails, then there is another way. Intellectual understanding and knowledge – that is, science – can effect the balances of opposing elements and resolve conflict. Knowledge, gained through time by painful and laborious trial and error, is power, and intellectual mastery leads to conquest and control.

The Romans were different from the Greeks in many fundamental ways, and one of the most fundamental was their view of nature and its forces. In the Homeric poems the anthropomorphic gods suggest a time when they were a way of seeing and understanding natural forces – Zeus with his commanding thunderbolt, Poseidon the Earthshaker as storm and earthquake, Aphrodite as sexuality. Then, of course, "the discovery of the mind" led to an entirely new way of understanding nature: Ionian philosophy became Aristotelian science. The Romans, though, instinctively and uniquely saw nature in terms of those fields they remained so close to and which had been so recently the entire focus of their lives. *Na-tura* is that which produces life and growth. The natural world (*ta physika* of the Greeks) is *rerum natura*: to translate it, as we inevitably do, "the nature of things" is to obscure entirely its significance, "that which brings into being our physical world." This *natura* was experienced, every day and at first hand, on the farm: there, and not in anthropomorphic divinities or in speculative philosophy or observational science, were to be seen the processes of life – birth, growth, struggle, decline, and death.

When Virgil left Arcadia and the Italianate pastoral landscape, as the pastoral shade and shadows descending on the mountainsides at the end of Eclogue 1 eventually became the shade harmful to both singers and crops in the epilogue to the whole collection (10.70–7), he turned from poetry that had the magician's power to transform reality, to the poetry of science, just as he turned from an imagined landscape to a real one. He abandoned the pastoral because of the ultimate failure of the imagination to create peace from a reality of war, but here, on the Italian farm, was an opportunity for a different sort of poetry, here knowledge and understanding could control warring opposites to achieve productive balance and harmony. If this explains how and why Virgil conceived of a poem on farming as the book of pastoral poems was taking its final form as a whole, it does not make sufficiently clear what an extraordinary conception this really was – so unexpected and original in subject and genre, so perfectly suited as a Roman exploration of the current Roman experience.

We can do no more than skim over the surface of this poem, following certain contours that will lead us to the *Aeneid*. The first three books cover the usual subjects of handbooks of agriculture: Book I deals with field crops, II with fruit trees and vines, and III with herds and flocks; apiculture, the subject of Book IV, is not usually treated at such length as a separate topic. But in the progression of these books a far grander scheme becomes apparent. Book I looks at the universe, II descends to consider the earth and its lands, and III narrows the focus to living things; IV, almost a coda, finally presents an abstracted history of human society. In all this, though, the farmer is never forgotten.

The first book has, at first sight, a general resemblance to Hesiod's *Works and Days* and would appear to fall into two very unequal halves – the "works" of 43–203 and the "days" (that is, the farmer's astronomical calendar) of 204–514. The first half, though, has nothing to do with Hesiod but rather openly acknowledges and adapts the topics outlined in Varro's prose treatise, the *De re rustica*: (1) knowing the farm's situation and soil, (2) the necessary equipment, (3) what must be done, and (4) when it must be done. But in Virgil's treatment of Varro's topics of agriculture, the farm is transformed into the world itself, a microcosm of the warring forces and the elemental balances of the universe. To know one's land and how to work it is to know the macrocosm, and in the "days" half of the book the farmer becomes just such a participant in the workings of the universe. He must observe the annual cycle of the heavens and understand, through the collective knowledge of science (the *praecepta veterum*, "the teachings of our ancestors") how to work within it. We can now see the reason for the unbalanced halves, because a tripartite structure emerges. Just as the first half closes with the simile of the rower who must fight constantly against the current in order not to be swept back downstream, so there are two further closures, the great storm that destroys the farmer's efforts in spite of all (311–50) and the great storm of Roman civil war (464–514). The farmer's knowledge and labors cannot save his crops from storm, nor can we avert the destruction of civil war.

Having dealt with field crops, in Book II Virgil goes on to trees – vines (for the most part) and olives. In the first book the farmer had to know the universe – the heavens, the seasons, the times ordained by the stars in their annual progress. Book II comes down to earth: each land and each farm has its own character that must be recognized for what it is, for the vine and the olive require very different conditions. Sections of instruction are marked off again by three "digressions" (as they have been called), set pieces belonging to the rhetorical category of the *laudatio*, a speech of praise. We have the Praise of Italy (136–76), as a land of perfect balance and therefore of perfect bounty; the Praise of Spring (315–45), a time of balance between the seasons of cold and wet (winter) and hot and dry (summer) and therefore a season of quiet and of birth, when the earth itself in a primal spring produced life for the first time; and the Praise of Country Life, with which the book closes (458–540), with its idealized picture of the farmer, far from the madding crowd, who enjoys the peace, leisure, and bounty of a happy and co-operative nature. All is light and happiness in these three visions, until one looks more closely at the details, which reveal them to be lies – grand, glorious, and necessary, but lies nonetheless. Italy is a land of war, for instance. Spring is in fact, as the technical instruction of the book has been insisting, the time of storms, as is autumn, because then the fixed qualities of winter and summer meet and are in conflict (the great storm of Book I occurred in the spring). And, as we learn throughout the poem and have seen in Book I, the reality of the farmer's life, far from being an idyll of ease amid the bounty of nature, is struggle, endless labor, and inevitable defeat. The primary focus of the book is on the vine, which takes on repeated associations of war (the olive of peace, which requires little work, receives little attention). As the didactic content reaches its conclusion, we are hammered repeatedly and powerfully with the endless cycle of annual effort and violence required to produce wine, which becomes the object of "vituperation," the rhetorical opposite of the *laudatio*.

Book III narrows Virgil's focus still further, from the universe of Book I, to the earth of II, and now to the life upon it. Large animals (bovine and equine) are the subject of the first half, and small animals (ovine and caprine) of the second. This bipartite division sets up the ultimate opposition of war and peace, since horses (which receive more attention than cattle, just as the vine received more than the olive) are raised only for war. The shepherd's flocks take us immediately back to the artificial pastoral landscape of the *Eclogues*. Nothing Virgil wrote is richer, more poetically intricate, or more deeply moving than this book, to which a survey can do little justice. It is dominated by the element of fire. The fire of war is developed in the horse through breeding and training, but ultimately and inevitably, when taken to the extreme, it destroys all, becoming, in the grand and dire conclusion of this first half (242–83), the fire of sexual passion which nothing can withstand. "All creatures on earth, men, beasts of the wild, fish of the sea, flocks, and bright birds, rush to their destruction in the passion and fire of love's madness: for all creatures the power of love is one and the same" (*in furias ignemque ruunt: amor omnibus idem*, 3.242–4). The madness (*furor*) of war and sexuality (the "essential" identity of the two) will recur throughout the *Aeneid*: this is one of the instances of the influence of the *Aeneid* on the *Georgics*. The second half of Book III is a superb and subtle integration of the practical and didactic (the shepherd, of course, must find and produce the perfectly balanced environment for his flock) with the idealized pastoral (the cool shade by the water, rest and respite from the midday heat). Again, though, that *sine qua non* of the ideal pastoral world (its perpetual summer, its warmth and unclouded sun) is pushed to its extreme, and the book ends with the fire of the plague that leaves a barren wasteland behind it (478–566). It is important to note, as we follow the development of fire throughout the book, just how "essential" it is. It exists already in the horse most suited for war, needing only to be brought out by breeding and training, and it is of course the necessary given of summer pasturing. The madness and fire of sexual passion, and the accursed fire of plague (*sacer ignis*, 566), are not external forces of destruction coming from without, but are inherent and dominant in both animals and the landscape: it is important here to remember the Roman view of character (*ingenium*).

Here the Georgics end. Every time Virgil has had occasion to refer to the content of his poem he has done so by mentioning only fields, trees, and animals – only in the very beginning are bees included (1.4). He has covered the three major areas of agriculture and has shown us our place within the universe around us, our earth and that which grows upon it, and the nature of our animate being. We have seen, in Book I, storms (and other pests) gathering, raging, and destroying, which we might be able to predict but certainly cannot control; and we have seen, in Book III, very similar forces of destruction that would appear to lie entirely within us. In between, in Book II, we have those visions of peace, calm, quiet, and hope, visions that we may briefly experience and by which we must live, however flawed and unreal our experience and knowledge of the real world reveal them to be. The Georgics are complete, but of the *Georgics* there is one more book.

Apiculture was far more important in the ancient Mediterranean world than it is for us today, honey being then the only source of sucrose, but it does not appear that agricultural handbooks paid more attention to bees than they did to dogs or pack animals, and even less than to vegetable gardening. From Aristotle on, though, the hive had always been closely observed as a miniature of human society, organized under a king bee (not a queen) in recognizable social units, complete with armies and a remarkable division of communal labor. Book IV, then, as a distinct appendage, makes good sense: how else, at this point, could Virgil possibly have narrowed his focus still further to consider human society? But what sort of a consideration is this? Is it descriptive, and if so to what purpose? Is it prescriptive – a model to emulate, a plan for a just and happy society? Or is it simply Utopian, a grand design that can never be, short of a city in the sky? Further questions abound, still unsettled. Who, for instance, is the great beekeeper, who cares for these tiny and fragile creatures, who in fact creates their world for them, and in whose sight even their heroic battles are insignificant, so easily quieted by a handful of dust? Is he some rather un-Roman divinity? Or Octavian himself? Or is Octavian to be seen as one of the two king bees doing battle, with Antony as the other? There are so many questions, and as many answers as there are readers.

I can suggest, though, that if the paths laid down above offer sound footing, there may be a way in. Our beekeeper is none other than the farmer who has been receiving instruction all the way along, the inheritor of the knowledge and the wisdom of the ages (the *praecepta veterum*), whose scientific understanding of his world affords him control over it, producing, with constant effort, the fruits of the begrudging and untrustworthy earth – if, that is, storm or plague doesn't wipe out all his labors first. The beekeeper, then, is you, Virgil's Roman reader. It is you, who, as you read, create this paradigm of a human society, first creating for the bees a world in an ideal temperateness (4.8–50) much like the ideal of the world's first spring we read of in Book II, and then attracting and caring for this people (51–66), observing with the detached superiority of any reader the growth and progress – the history, in fact – of a people. This is no allegory, but Virgil has offered occasional suggestions and just enough nudging for you, the Roman reader and great beekeeper, to see some misty relevance to your own history: there were kings and glorious battles associated with your Trojan origin, so long ago and so filtered through Homer and epic legend that as stories, however exciting and moving, they have no more reality or immediacy than the spring battles between competing swarms of bees, so easily quelled (67–87). You can observe, though, as this people becomes more real to you, under your constant care and attention, that all may not be well, that there are real human passions there, given to them by Jupiter as their inborn character (149–52). Sexual passion may have been absent, as it were, at an early stage in the history of these Quirites (as they are called, 201), when the whole people worked only for the common good (153–209), as is your conception of the glorious period after the expulsion of the last king (so simple an act when you read of it in books of history, just as easy as pulling the wings off a king bee). At that time, it seemed, there was indeed divinity within them (219–27). But the bees are exposed to all the ills to which we are heir (228–50) – disease especially, which can destroy them utterly, no matter what you may do to prevent or cure (251–80).

What I think Virgil has given us here is a universal history, from the beginning of the human race to the Rome of his own day, written directly for the Roman reader when a terrible disease seemed to be destroying the whole people (as Livy too, among others, was to view it in his *Praefatio*). There is a certain chronology apparent here, I think, sufficient to suggest the historical narrative promised in the book's statement of subject (4.3–5), with occasional digressions on human nature and on the character of this particular people, as would be expected in a history. If we read these panels *chronologically*, as representations of the traditional stages of Roman history, then the obvious and troubling contradictions about the nature of the bees disappear, for we are seeing *a development, not a sociology of a people at a particular point in time.* But what is most striking in all this is Virgil's view of history, of what history means, not as a subject of antiquarian study, but for its relevance for a people at a time of crisis, because it is this compelling need to understand Rome's past that led him on to the *Aeneid*. Here again it seems as if the *Aeneid* offers an extended commentary on these passages, rather than the other way around.

The second half of Book IV is a poem in itself, of a very different sort. If the apicultural instruction is not a coherent and necessary part of the georgic instruction of the first three books but is to be seen as a summation or abstraction, then the second half of the book is a further poetic abstraction. The subject of disease, wiping out the entire swarm, leads to the proposition of a fabulous remedy, the *bougonia*, and that leads to the story of the discoverer of the remedy, Aristaeus. Within Aristaeus' story is the panel of Orpheus and Eurydice, a structure similar to Catullus' epyllion, poem 64, in which the embedded story offers thematic amplification, comment, and even explanation of the surrounding panel. The Orpheus story is clearly about loss, triumph, and ultimate failure. Orpheus is a poet-magician (a *vates*), whose song is magic because it can control nature and overcome even death itself, as he wins back Eurydice from death and the Underworld. Orpheus is also a poet-scientist, as he was in the *Eclogues*, where he is represented as the semi-divine counterpart to the Alexandrians Conon and Aratus (on the cups at *Ecl.* 3.40–6) and as the predecessor of Hesiod (*Ecl.* 6.70–1). Science and magic in the *Georgics* are the same – the knowledge that can control nature and lead to ultimate power. But Orpheus, though triumphant, loses Eurydice and everything else as he turns, driven by *furor*, to look back at her. That forbidden glance is the single thing that is beyond his control.

Aristaeus is a figure created largely by Virgil to be the semi-divine discoverer of agriculture, as a figure of science something of a doublet to
Orpheus. He claims, in fact, to have discovered, through trial and experience, the subjects of Books I, II, and III (4.326–32). The loss of his swarm,
then, is another failure of science, of the power of knowledge. He too, like
Orpheus, then triumphs over death: he is sent to wrestle with the seer
Proteus, overcoming him by violent force as Proteus changes shapes, even
becoming the elemental fire and water. Victorious, Aristaeus wins the
secret of the *bougonia*, the rebirth of the swarm from the putrescent
innards of a bullock ritually slaughtered. But does Aristaeus succeed,
where Orpheus had failed? Are we to understand that science (the control
of our world through the knowledge won by similar wrestling) actually
does contain our redemption, the rebirth of a people all but annihilated
by disease?

We must realize clearly from the start that the *bougonia* is something
completely unreal. No one had ever done this, because it simply can't be
done, as Virgil knew perfectly well. In any case, no farmer in his right mind
in the real world would ever even think of sacrificing a valuable bullock
(much less four, as Aristaeus finally does) to get in return a swarm of bees.
We are in the world of fairy tale here, as Virgil repeatedly makes clear: this
is a *thauma*, a wonder never intended as something to be believed, a
marvel like flying snakes or a two-headed, talking calf. But to point out
what is both obvious and prosaic is by no means a dismissal of this marvel
with which Virgil has chosen to close his poem. It is only to see it for what
it is – a wonderful image of regeneration, even if totally unreal.

For Virgil there were two ways of making sense of the chaos of his world,
two sorts of poetic understanding. In the grand conclusion of Book II (the
Praise of Country Life), he expresses his wish that the Muses receive him
and teach him science (2.475–82), but if he is incapable of that sort of
understanding, then he hopes to be happy in the country, inglorious,
among the streams, woods, and shade (483–9). "Blessed is he who can
understand the workings of nature," he says, "and overcome all fears and
even death, but happy too is he who knows the rural gods" (490–4). Elsewhere in the *Georgics*, too, Virgil has recalled the poetic mode of the
Eclogues, the imaginative transformation of reality by the singer in the
shade of that idealized landscape, where every loss and all pain can be
cured by the medicine of song. We saw, though, the ultimate failure of this
vision in the face of reality, and we have seen throughout the *Georgics* the
failure, too, of science. We must create images to live by – images of rural
peace, of the easy bounty of a co-operative nature, of Italy as a land of
perfect balances and fertility, of pastoral ease, of country gods to whom
we need only pray. But even in these visions of hope Virgil continually

includes inescapable reminders of reality. There *are* snakes in Italy, and in the shepherd's shady rest, and in the grass of the river bank where Eurydice was fleeing from Aristaeus' human passion: *latet anguis in herba* (*Ecl.* 3.93) might well be the epigraph for all of Virgil. Scientific understanding fails too: we may be able to predict the storms of spring and of civil war, if we learn to observe the signs, but we are powerless to withstand them, nor can we keep *furor* in check. Orpheus – poet, magician, and scientist – conquering even death, was no more able to withstand *furor* than was Gallus dying in Arcadia, whose final words stand as the sum of the *Eclogues*: *'omnia vincit Amor: et nos cedamus Amori'* (*Ecl.* 10.69). Eurydice's final words to Orpheus have a similar finality: "What is this that has destroyed us both, Orpheus, what is this madness of human passion, so overwhelming?" (*illa, 'quis et me' inquit 'miseram et te perdidit, Orpheu,/quis tantus furor?'*, *Geo.* 4.494–5).

Appendix: The Latin Hexameter

(Knowledge of the basic principles of Latin accentuation and of the scansion of the dactylic hexameter is assumed.)

Spoken Latin had two sources of rhythm: word accent and the succession of long and short syllables. (In this, modern Italian is similar, having both word accent and well-defined syllabic length.) Latin verse is an entirely natural combination, or exploitation, of both sources of rhythm.

Word Accent

That Latin had a word accent (stress) has been questioned and even denied by modern scholars. (Classical Greek had a pitch accent rather than a stress accent, and modern French, for instance, has a phrase accent, and both these systems have led to doubts about the Latin word accent.) Linguistic evidence, though, seems conclusive, and there is no good reason to question the usual grammar-book rules.

For example, vowels in accented syllables resisted change, whereas those in unstressed syllables tended to weaken in various ways (e.g. *déxtĕra > déxtra, ávĭceps > aúceps, mŏ́dō > mŏ́dŏ, bĕ́nē > bĕ́nĕ* – the last two examples by the "rule of iambic shortening," which assumes word accent). In early (pre-Plautine) Latin the initial syllable of a word was accented: this explains the weakening of the vowel in such words as *capio* and *facio* in compounds, when the *-a-*, unprotected by accent, changed to the more colorless *-i-* (*pércipio, ínterficio*).

In reading Latin verse it is important to preserve the normal accent of every word (though in the early stages of learning to read hexameters it may be impossible, or counterproductive, to try to observe word accent).

No Roman would accent the final syllables of *canó* and *Troiáe* when reading the first line of the *Aeneid*, any more than we would accept a line of verse that forced us to pronounce "Mílwaukée" or "Minnéapolís."

Verse Ictus

Every syllable of a Latin word was either long or short, depending on the actual length of time it took to pronounce it. Long vowels were held out, short vowels were not. A syllable closed by two consonants took longer to pronounce than an open syllable or one closed by a single consonant. (For example, in the nominative *pŭ-ēll-ă*, the first and third syllables would be of minimal duration, but the second, with the double consonant articulated properly, would be – theoretically, at least – twice as long.)

Latin verse is "quantitative" because it depends on the regular succession of long and short syllables. In the dactylic hexameter, this means either ‒◡◡ or ‒‒ as the basic units of rhythm. In each of these two feet, the constant element is the first syllable (always long), whereas the second element is variable. It is the constant element that establishes the pattern we hear as rhythm, as, for example, the rhythm of the first line of the *Aeneid*:

‒◡◡ | ‒◡◡ | ‒‒ | ‒‒ | ‒◡◡ | ‒‒

Now, it is crucial that we realize that this rhythm is totally independent of accents or beats or stresses of any sort. The pattern would be apparent even if played on an electric telegraph key, on which every tone must be of exactly the same intensity. But for us (speakers of English, at least) it is extremely difficult, and perhaps impossible, to hear this rhythm without bringing to it a stress on the first long of each foot (the constant element), since all our aural rhythm is accentual, whether in verse or in music. Thus, when we learn to read Latin hexameters, we make two fatal, though inevitable, errors: (1) we import a stress or beat that should not be there, and (2) we mispronounce Latin words by misplacing normal word accent (e.g., *canó* and *Troiáe*).

Accent and Ictus

If, however, we can maintain the flow of dactyls and spondees, giving full time to the long syllables and less to the short (though not, of course, with the monotonous regularity of a metronome), avoiding adding any stress or beat to the beginning of each foot, and if we observe normal word accent, we then hear clearly the wonderful interplay between the "ictus" wave and the tension and release imposed upon it by word accent – not just one rhythm, but really two.

If one reads down the right-hand side of any page of the *Aeneid*, it is obvious that, with very few exceptions, in the last two feet of each line word accent corresponds with, and thus reinforces, the verse ictus – that is, the word accent falls on the first long of each foot.

In the first four feet of each line, however, two (at least) will usually have a clash between the word accent and the verse ictus – that is, the word accent does not fall on the first long of the foot; for example,

Ǐtali|ǎm fa|tǒ profu|gǔs La|víniaque | vénit.
(*Aen.* 1.2)

This gives the Latin hexameter an audible tension in the first part of the line that is resolved at the end. Furthermore, the end of each line is clearly heard (as it isn't, for instance, in a succession of English iambic pentameters), not just because each line usually ends dactyl–spondee, but because these two feet are marked by the coincidence of accent and ictus.

Caesura and Diaeresis

Caesura ("a cutting") is the term for word end within a foot.

Diaeresis is the term for word end corresponding with the end of a foot.

Every word, therefore, will produce either a caesura or a diaeresis. Why, then, does either matter? We are told that every hexameter line has a "main" or "principal" caesura, usually to be found in the third foot, and that this caesura is either the "strong" (or "masculine") caesura, occurring after the first long of the foot (‒ || ‿‿ or ‒ || ‒), or the "weak" (or "feminine"), after the first short of a dactyl (‿‿ || ‿). We are never told why all this is so, except perhaps that the hexameter line is so long that it requires some sort of pause near the middle, or that the main caesura can also mark a break in sense. Such explanations seem either vague or arbitrary: certainly the hexameter is not an unusually long line, and it takes only a few minutes of reading to see that this "main" caesura doesn't consistently coincide with any real break or even a pause in the sense of a line.

The Third-Foot Caesura

In the Greek hexameter, from Homer on, there is normally a caesura in the third foot, with the weak preferred to the strong. Quintus Ennius (239–169

BC) was the first poet at Rome to use the Greek dactylic hexameter, but although he imitated many features of Homeric style as well as he could in Latin, he made one major metrical change: more than 8 of every 10 of his hexameter lines have a strong caesura in the third foot, and the percentage is even higher (more than 9 of 10) in later hexameter poets.

Latin had something that Greek did not, and that was a marked word accent. This accent never fell on the final syllable of a word. It is obvious, then, that if a word of two or more syllables ends after the first long of a foot (that is, producing a strong caesura), there will be a clash between accent and ictus in that foot (. . . | $\overset{\text{x}}{-}$ ‖). Ennius, who was famously trilingual (Greek, Latin, and Oscan), must have realized immediately that its word accent gave Latin a rhythmical potential that Greek did not have – that he could create in his hexameter line a tension caused by the conflict of accent and ictus in the first part of the line that could be resolved at the end. This tension is guaranteed by a third-foot strong caesura, whereas a weak caesura (the more common one in Greek) produces coincidence of accent and ictus (. . . | $\acute{-}$ ⌣).

The regular occurrence of a strong caesura in the third foot, then, is an entirely *secondary, metrical phenomenon*. It is the result of the clash of accent and ictus in the third foot, and is *natural* (that is, in no way artificial) and *audible*.

The First Foot

Conflict of accent and ictus in the first foot is harder to obtain. If the line begins with a monosyllabic, spondaic, trochaic, or dactylic word, there cannot be conflict (that is, word accent must fall on the initial long):

[-] . . . ,   e.g. *ví superum* (*Aen.* 1.4)
[--] . . . ,   e.g. *Tróas* (1.30)
[-⌣] . . . ,   e.g. *árma* (1.1)
[-⌣⌣] . . . ,   e.g. *lítora* (1.3)

Conflict will occur, then, only if the first word of the line is trisyllabic, of three long syllables (a "molossus"), or tetrasyllabic, beginning with a dactyl (a "choriamb"):

[---] . . . ,   e.g. $\overset{\text{x}}{i}$*nsignem* (1.10)
[-⌣⌣-] . . . ,   e.g. $\overset{\text{x}}{I}$*taliam* (1.2)

(There are only a few other possibilities.)

The Hexameter Line

The majority of hexameter lines, then, will begin, in theory, with coincidence of accent and ictus in the first foot, and this can be confirmed by a quick look at any page of the *Aeneid*. If the intention of Latin poets was to secure as much conflict as possible in the first four feet, with the resulting tension, then the second and fourth feet, as well as the third, will inevitably have strong caesurae.

The following examples (taken mostly from Book I) will illustrate some of the effects achieved. Virgil composed by ear, not according to any set of rules such as those found in handbooks of meter, and if his lines are read with attention to the quantitative rhythm and normal word accents, the special effects can easily be heard.

To begin at the beginning, consider first

* árma vi|rúmque ca|nŏ̆, Troi|ăe qui | prímus ab | óris.*

(1.1)

There are two important points to notice here. (1) The first two words proclaim "*Iliad*" and "*Odyssey*" and introduce a *Leitmotif* resounding throughout the poem, and hence both words are emphasized by coincidence of accent and ictus. (2) But because there is no conflict in the first two feet, tension must be secured by conflict in the third (with the expected strong caesura) and in the fourth. Why did Virgil displace the relative pronoun *qui*, writing *Troiae qui* . . . instead of (the normal) *qui Troiae* . . . ? Quite obviously because this achieves conflict in the fourth foot, which . . . *qui* | *Troíae* . . . does not.

The extraordinary effectiveness of the two lines describing Dido's appearance as she mounts her pyre is in large measure the result of both the tension and the emphasis inherent in the Latin hexameter:

sănguine|ăm vŏl|vĕns ăci|ĕm, măcu|llĭsquĕ tre|méntis
ınter|fusa ge|nás et | pállida | morte fu|ltura.

(4.643–4)

There is the maximum possible tension in the first four feet of 643, but in 644 only the third foot (with its normal strong caesura) has a conflict, resulting in the emphatic coincidences stressing the adjectives *interfusa* and *pallida*.

The storm in Book I wrecks Orontes' ship and crew:

appa|rent ra|rī nan|tēs in | gurgite | vasto.

(1.118)

Here too (as in 4.643) there is maximum tension (conflict in the first four feet), emphasized, moreover, by the four successive spondees.

Conversely, as in 4.644, maximum coincidence can be exploited for emphasis, as in Juno's ringing and insistent command to Aeolus:

incute | vim ven|tīs sub | mersasque | obrue | puppes.

(1.69)

Her whole speech to Aeolus is notable for its rhythmical directness, hammering away as if it were prose (I do not mean "prosaic"). Of its 11 lines, 10 begin with coincidence in the first foot, and in 8 the coincidence extends to the second foot. To describe the effect in these terms can easily give the wrong impression: this is something Virgil heard, and this is the way he wanted Juno's words to sound – he did not have to calculate the instances of coincidence, and neither should we.

Similarly, we can hear the power of the storm winds in a line that is entirely dactylic (in contrast to the spondees of 1.118, above):

in vada | caeca tu|līt peni|tusque pro|cacibus | Austris.

(1.536)

Consider now four lines in which emphasis is given by coincidence in the third foot – that is, lines that do not have the expected strong caesura in that foot. As the storm breaks, Aeneas speaks for the first time in the poem, ending with the *Leitmotif* "arms and the man:"

scuta vi|rum gale|asque et | fortia | corpora | volvit.

(1.101)

We hear it again just a few lines later,

arma vi|rum tabu|laeque et | Troia | gaza per | undas.

(1.119)

In both of these lines the only conflict is in the second foot, and the emphasis resulting from the normal word accents is audible, and in no way artificially contrived. Similarly audible is the emphasis of Jupiter's words to Venus, admitting Juno's interference,

quaé mare | núnc ter|rásque me|tú cae|lúmque fa|tīgat,
(1.280)

where the only conflict is in the fourth foot. This line is, in fact, the second of two successive lines with coincidence in the third foot: Jupiter has just proclaimed,

ímperi|úm sine | fíne de|dī . . . ,
(1.279)

thereby establishing, with metrical emphasis, the permanence of Roman power.

These last four lines are, of course, examples of weak caesurae in the third foot, which necessarily produce coincidence of accent and ictus. This infrequent caesura (less than 1 of every 10 lines) is employed purposefully by Virgil, either for emotional emphasis (as above), or at the beginning of a prayer, or to convey the flavor of Greek poetry.

When Aeneas addresses his men after the storm, he begins with emphasis on their previous sufferings,

ó pas|sí gravi|óra, da|bít deus | hís quoque | fínem.
(1.199)

This caesura can support an entirely different sort of emotion, though, as a result of its release of the expected tension in the third foot:

et iam nox umida caelo
práecipi|tát sua|déntque ca|déntia | sídera | somnos,
(2.8–9)

which is repeated

lumenque obscura vicissim
lúna pre|mít sua|déntque ca|déntia | sídera | somnos,
(4.80–1)

a line with only one conflict.

Prayers are the expression of direct emotion, and in Latin poetry they very frequently begin with a weak caesura in the third foot, as does the prayer of Aeneas when he suspects that the Libyan huntress might be some goddess:

sís fel|íx nos|trúmque le|vés, quae|cúmque la|bórum.
                                                                (1.330)

Examples are numerous, but the most significant and grand is Aeneas'
solemn invocation at the ritual of treaty in Book XII, beginning

ésto | núnc Sol | téstis et | haéc mihi | térra vo|cánti,
                                                                (12.176)

a line with complete coincidence of accent and ictus.

The third-foot weak caesura was the most common in Greek hexameters, and Latin poets often use it to suggest something Greek, sometimes
simply with a Greek proper name, as in Jupiter's first words to Venus,

párce me|tú, Cyther|éa, ma|nént im|móta tu|órum.
                                                                (1.257)

The effect of a Homeric line is often reinforced by this caesura, as, for
example,

Ánthea | Sérge|stúmque vi|dét for|témque Clo|ánthum.
                                                                (1.510)

Dido, entering the temple with her entourage in Book I, is compared to
Diana pre-eminent among her nymphs, an important simile making the
connection with Nausicaa among her maids (*Od.* 6.102–9); Virgil cites his
Homeric model with a line that not only has the weak caesura in the third
foot, but is entirely without conflict of accent and ictus,

hínc atque | hínc glome|rántur O|réades; | ílla pha|rétram.
                                                                (1.500)

When Venus abandons her son, turning from him, a true goddess, and
departs to her Greek temple on Paphos, both her sublimity and her Greek
retreat are metrically significant:

ípsa Pa|phím sub|límis ab|ít se|désque re|vísit.
                                                                (1.415)

Venus in her huntress get-up is like the Thracian Harpalyce:

Hárpaly|cé volu|crémque fu|gá prae|vértitur | Hébrum.
                                                                (1.317)

This line is typical of the use of a weak caesura in a context of Greek proper names and allusion, but what is most unusual is that the entire description of Venus as huntress – all six lines, 315–20 – have the third-foot weak caesura. Again, this effect is entirely audible and would have been obvious to any Roman reader: it is not only Venus' costume that is outlandish.

The Catullan Molossus

There is one further metrical feature that is worth noting here, both as an excellent example of how suggestive a seemingly small stylistic detail can be, and because it would have been, to the Roman ear, entirely audible. One notable mannerism of Catullus in his epyllion, poem 64, is the placement of a word of three long syllables (a "molossus") before the bucolic diaeresis (word end after the fourth foot), as in the first line of poem 64,

Peliaco quondam prōgnātāe | vertice pinus.

Of the first 21 lines of the poem, 12 have this mannerism, and Catullus will use it repeatedly in successive lines, often with a verb as the molossus, and often with nouns and their modifiers elegantly disposed around the verb (as in the so-called "golden line"), e.g.

rura colit nemo, mōllēscūnt | colla iuvencis,
non humilis curvis pūrgātūr | vinea rastris,
non glaebam prono cōnvēllīt | vomere taurus.
(64.38–40)

There are five such lines in succession at 86–90, four at 187–90, and other sequences of three (e.g. 233–5, 314–16). This rhythm says "Catullus" just as unmistakably, and as audibly, as the opening chords of the Fifth Symphony say "Beethoven."

Virgil used this feature in a characteristic way, not just to recall Catullus, but to evoke the central premise of his epyllion, the crucial turning point in human history when, with the sailing of the Argo and its heroes, the happy collaboration between gods and men came to a sudden end and warfare, greed, violence, and immorality became the human lot. A single line of Jupiter's speech to Venus in Book I brings all this to mind (see above, p. 117):

aspera tum positis mītēscēnt | saecula bellis.
(1.291)

In a similar and obviously related prophecy, Eclogue 4 (the "Messianic" Eclogue), Virgil imagines the process of Catullus' devolution in reverse, tracing the return of human society gradually from the present to a future golden age, as the Parcae of Catullus 64 sing a new wedding song (4.46–7). When Virgil touches upon the deeds of heroes (*heroum laudes*, 4.26), there are three lines of golden age idealism:

> *molli paulatim flāvēscēt | campus arista*
> *incultisque rubens pēndēbīt | sentibus uva*
> *et durae quercus sūdābūnt | roscida mella.*
>   (4.28–30)

General Index

Index of Passages

Printed in the United States
204140BV00006B/10-24/P